MUSIC AND ITS SOCIAL MEANINGS

MUSICOLOGY SERIES
Edited by F. Joseph Smith

Volume 1   THE EXPERIENCING OF MUSICAL SOUND
Prelude to a Phenomenology of Music
F. Joseph Smith

Volume 2   MUSIC AND ITS SOCIAL MEANINGS
Christopher Ballantine

Additional volumes in preparation

ISSN 0275 5866
This book is part of a series. The publishers will accept continuation orders which may be cancelled at any time and which provide automatic billing and shipping of each title in the series upon publication. Please write for details.

MUSIC AND ITS SOCIAL MEANINGS

by
Christopher Ballantine
University of Natal

GORDON AND BREACH SCIENCE PUBLISHERS

New York   London   Paris   Montreux   Tokyo

Copyright © 1984 Gordon and Breach, Science Publishers, Inc.

Gordon and Breach Science Publishers

One Park Avenue
New York, NY 10016
United States of America

42 William IV Street
London WC2N 4DE
England

58, rue Lhomond
75005 Paris
France

P. O. Box 161
1820 Montreux-2
Switzerland

48-2 Minamidama, Oami Shirasato-machi
Sambu-gun
Chiba-ken 299-32
Japan

Library of Congress Cataloging in Publication Data
Ballantine, Christopher John.
    Music and its social meanings.

    (Monographs on musicology, ISSN 0275—5866; v.2)
    1. Music.and society. 2. Music—Philosophy and aesthetics. I. Title. II. Series: Monographs on music; v2.
ML3795.B28   1983   780'.07   82-9314
ISBN 0-677-06050-5

For the Memory of My Mother;
For My Father;
And for Diana

CONTENTS

Introduction
by Wilfred Mellers   ix

Preface   xv

Acknowledgements   xix

I   Music and Society: The Forgotten Relationship   1

II   Beethoven, Hegel and Marx   30

III   Social and Philosophical Outlook in Mozart's
      Operas   49

IV   Charles Ives and the Meaning of Quotation in
      Music   72

V   A Musical Triptych: The Contemporary Scene   92

VI   An Aesthetic of Experimental Music   107

VII   A Revaluation of Sibelius' Symphonies   134

      Index   197

Introduction

I was recently invited to address a conference on Change and Revolution in the Education of Musicians in Society. The formulation seemed odd to me, for what musicians are not 'in society'? It turned out that professional musicians were considered to be asocial types; 'musicians in society' meant ordinary folk. Since the conference was an international gathering of music educators I found this formulation (which has since been changed) depressing: for it suggested that the organisers were to some degree moulded by the perverse view of the nature of music which, as educators, they should have been combating. In Western society we have for a long time lived with the notion that music is, in more senses than one, a mystery, a private language and a skill which only those endowed by God with musical talent fostered by years of technical application have the right to 'understand'. Having arrived at such a conclusion, it is only one further step to an attitude whereby understanding is itself deplored. All that matters is the Mystery, which must remain sacrosanct.

The historical reasons for this are too complex to be discussed here, though Christopher Ballantine touches on many of them in this book. But the basic psychological and philosophical reasons seem to me to stem from 'Western' man's *fear*. As his intellect grew increasingly comprehensive and his 'scientific' mastery of facts more redoubtable, so he increasingly came to distrust the un- or sub-conscious workings of his mind, which inevitably threatened that mastery. Yet it is precisely these areas of experience with which the arts, and especially music, have always been concerned. So because he was afraid of them, Modern Man pretended that they didn't exist: as is exemplified as early as the late eighteenth century in Dr. Burney's inanely complacent definition of music as 'an Innocent Luxury, unnecessary indeed to our Existence, but a great

Improvement and gratification of the Sense of Hearing'. How that definition would have appalled Bach, who believed that music was 'a harmonious euphony for the glory of God and the instruction of my neighbour'; or Beethoven, who rightly maintained that he who *truly* understands my music will be freed thereby from all the miseries of the world' (my italics). How for that matter it would have appalled the 'savages' of the Australian Bush or 'darkest Africa', or even the Eskimos in their frozen wastes, all of whom believe music to be not a titillating excrescence, but an activity without which life might literally cease. For without it the sun could not provoke fecundity nor the moon control the tides. History demonstrates from the dark backward abysm of time to the precarious present, that music, far from being 'unnecessary to our existence', is a need as vital as bread: perhaps more so, since whereas an individual would die without food, without music a whole society, perhaps even the cosmos itself, might disintegrate.

Of course 'academic' musicians today wouldn't admit that they subscribe to Dr. Burney's view of music's nature and purpose; they would claim that they 'understand' Bach and Beethoven and have special qualifications for doing só. Nonetheless, many of them *act* as if they accepted Burney's concept. Musicologists in particular—those trained to discuss in technical terms the ways in which music functions—often insist so strongly on the hermeticism of their discipline that they distrust any attempt to trace the relationships between a sequence of musical events and their physiological and psychological conseqences. Yet that such relationships must exist is surely self-evident, since music is made by human beings. Put thus simply (not crudely), the case seems unanswerable; and the pretence that there is some 'purely' musical truth existing in a limbo uncontaminated by human contact seems both craven and contemptible.

In any case I—who have myself tried to write about music as the creation of human beings—salute in Christopher Ballantine a man who writes with intelligence and lucidity about the 'meanings' of music; who has no doubt that works of art make sense both intrinsi- cally and in the context of history; and who believes that music's meanings may be revealed only through the behaviour of music *per se*. His essay on the symphonies of Sibelius, for instance, starts from the technical legacy that Sibelius as symphonist inherited from Beethoven; yet in analysing the ways in which Sibelius extends the formal discoveries of Beethoven he reveals, firstly, the relation of Hegelian dialectic to the Beethovenian concept of the symphony, and, secondly, the further psychological (and ultimately sociological) changes inherent in the 'morphological' forms which Sibelius explored under the impact of Beethoven's last works. Ballantine's essay is in the profoundest sense revelatory; formal process is a discovery of human identity and therefore of social purpose.

Similarly, at what seems to be a more overtly sociological level, Ballantine writes of the human motivations that, in a rapidly changing world, went to create Mozart's mature tragi-comic operas. But his analysis explores the central themes—the relation between mask and reality, the interdependence of positive and negative forces, the dialectic of forgiveness—not merely in terms of theatrical events, but simultaneously in terms of the inner life of the music: the interaction and fusion of the old 'closed' forms of opera seria, apposite to a closed society, with the 'open' forms of sonata, apposite to an evolutionary world. Closely connected with this, he writes of *why* we should honour Beethoven more than one-hundred-and-fifty years after his death: not because books tells us he was a Great Composer whose music we passively listen to in concert halls, as we look at visual artefacts in a museum, but because through his music he helped to make us what we are. History may have been made on the fields of Waterloo but the battle, Beethoven believed, was really taking place in his mind. He was right; and Ballantine shows us how and why.

At what some might think is the furthest possible extreme from this Beethoven essay Ballantine discusses the polarity of opposites between avant-garde music and experimental music. The work of the avant-garde became aurally unintelligible because its creators, for historically understandable if not altogether valid reasons, were no longer concerned with the post-Renaissance concept of music as communication, at least in a social context. So a counterpoise to the avant-garde emerged, experimental music, arbitrarily assembled from inchoate noises whether or not electrophonically processed, since in demanding participation from the musically trained and untrained alike it aimed to revive concepts that had withered with the scientific revolution. *Through* the science of electronics, human beings may be blindly or deafly hitting back at a world they didn't know they had made; and although their millings around may be more primitive than anything created by 'savages' (who *mean* something when they yell), it may not be entirely false to suggest that chaos is a necessary stage towards rebirth. This is also why Ballantine is interested in the demotic genres of music, hearing in jazz and some forms of rock (pre-eminently in Dylan) a growth from reborn childhood towards what he not extravagantly calls a tragic view of life. This is something which we who consider ourselves adult ought to be aware of, the more so because our electric-plastic age has also produced the phenomenon of Muzak—an inversion of music's essentially human nature, since it is not meant to be listened to.

Though this book is a collection of miscellaneous essays, it adumbrates a world-view of music's history. That view is Marxist, though Ballantine is not a Marxist who wears blinkers; nor does he think he knows all the answers. His Marxism illuminates, opens vistas, explores depths. Only very occasionally do I spot a sentence wherein doctrine seems to belie his exceptional intelligence. For instance, at the end of the Sibelius essay, he suggests that the composer's thirty-year-long silence after the Seventh Symphony was attributable to the fact that he betrayed himself by composing a march for the Lapua movement—'a conspiracy of capitalist interests to bring about a form of fascist dictatorship in Finland'. Of course Sibelius's life-long struggle with symphonic form *was* related to his concern with his country's struggle for political freedom. But no-one who has read and digested Ballantine's brilliant essay could believe that it is what Sibelius's symphonies are fundamentally about: any more than, in Beethoven's late music, the search for the whole within the divided self was primarily political in motivation. Though divisions within the human psyche had and still have political complements, I suspect that both Beethoven and Sibelius gave up the struggle to create a 'better' world materially, because they came to realize that any such better world was dependent on the re-creation of the 'whole' human being: a preoccupation which I along with Blake would call 'religious'. I find it as difficult to imagine a worldly panacea that would abolish human imperfection—pride, greed, sloth, jealousy, fear—as I do to imagine a Christian heaven in any harp-plucking physical embodiment. I'm not sure if Christopher Ballantine, a man as courageous as he is clever, foresees any such panacea; at least in one sense he offers us a foretaste, for he writes, as the phrase has it, 'like an angel'.

WILFRED MELLERS

University of York

Preface

The cognition of music languishes today in a condition which Adorno called 'inane isolation', utterly severed from an understanding of the concrete social conditions of music's genesis, as well as of those of its reception. While the analytical dissecting of musical compositions was, in Adorno's words, 'learning to trace the most delicate ramifications of the facture' and while musicological investigation was 'accounting at length for the biographical circumstances of composer and work, the method of deciphering the specific social characteristics of music has lagged pitifully'.[1] In the capitalist countries, serious and sustained attempts at such social deciphering of musical works are — with the unique and remarkable exception of Adorno — virtually nonexistent; more than that, such efforts are vigorously discouraged by the positivist orientation of the professional musical establishment. In those countries which have abolished capitalism, a social cognition of music is fostered but tends to founder in one of two kinds of methodological impasse: that of mechanistic and literalistic interpretation, and that of a simple and sterile juxtaposition of music and social exegesis.

This is the benighted context in which the essays in this volume have come into being. As such, they bear the wounds, the deformations, that inescapably accompany a project objectively so much in its infancy. It must be stressed here that the social interpretation of music to which I refer — the genuine sociology of *music* — is to be clearly distinguished from the empiricist forms of inquiry that proliferate under its name: these should more precisely be termed the sociology of musical life, or even the social history of

---

[1]   T.W. Adorno: *Introduction to the Sociology of Music* (trans. E.B. Ashton), New York, 1976, p.62.

musical life. What the sociology of music undertakes, by contrast, is (to draw upon Adorno's terminology) an investigation of the ways in which social formations crystallize in musical structures, indeed even in their inmost cells.[2] But this inquiry does not rely on the mere drawing of correspondences, since the process of crystallization is never simple or straightforward. On the contrary, it depends on a complex dialectic, in which elements of the social realm are mediated by the work in a manner which necessarily articulates some kind of social *response* to them. This engagement — which necessarily involves some form of selection, construction, or reconstruction — may be more critical or less, more acquiescent or less, more ideological or less, passive or active: these differences imply varieties of social perspective and social value. And it is here that the sociology of music reveals its inseparability from musical aesthetics. For the sociology of music does not rest content with an analysis of the music's own technical operations and a deciphering of the specific modes of response embedded in them: it also raises questions — themselves socially constituted — about the appropriateness of these technical operations and these modes of response, just as it wants to assesss the relationship between them.

The reasons why the cognition of music is so backward are not hard to discover. They include, for instance, both the notorious 'abstractness' of music's language, and the highly developed but narrow professionalism of the musical establishment. But by far the most important reason is that the separation of music from its social context, the artificial insulation of musical understanding from the realms of social meaning and value encoded in musical works, serves *ideological interests.* This insulation usually takes the form of a repression, or of a mystification — frequently working hand in hand. The struggle against these ideological distortions is a constant theme of the essays in this book, and the starting point of more than one of them. Perhaps the most obvious example is the essay on Beethoven, which found its impetus in the astonishing manner in which the official Beethoven anniversary celebrations of

---

[2]   T.W. Adorno: 'Theses on the Sociology of Art' (trans. Brian Trench), *Working Papers in Cultural Studies: 2,* Birmingham, Spring 1972, p. 125 (cf. also p. 128); and Adorno: *op. cit.,* p.70.

1970 paid obsequious tribute to the composer while at the very same time doing everthing that needed to be done to occlude the real significance of his music. Adorno speaks of this problem in a passage that could very well stand as an epigraph to that essay:

> If we listen to Beethoven and do not hear anything of the revolutionary bourgeoisie — not the echo of its slogans, the need to realize them, the cry for that totality in which reason and freedom are to have their warrant — we understand Beethoven no better than does one who cannot follow the purely musical content of his pieces, the inner history that happens to their themes. If so many dismiss that specifically social element as a mere additive of sociological interpretation, if they see the thing itself in the actual notes alone, this is not due to the music but to a neutralized consciousness. The musical experience has been insulated from the experience of the reality in which it finds itself — however polemically — and to which it responds.[3]

The 'neutralized consciousness' of which Adorno speaks is not simply a consciousness neutralized in relation to music; it is above all the false and ideological consciousness which arises out of and is actively propagated by the dominant class interests of advanced capitalist society. And although the essays in this volume address specifically and explicitly the problem of this neutralized *musical* consciousness in a number of its pertinent contemporary appearances, their ultimate — but implicit — target is the ideology through whose sway the present order reproduces itself. As such, the essays collaborate *with* the critical and emancipatory impulses of the musical works they discuss, and inveigh *against* the ossified, co-opted and repressed reproduction and consumption of this music. They rail therefore against all musical commodotization, musical reification, and musical mystification. They aim, as did Walter Benjamin, to rescue from the fate of oblivion which incessantly threatens works of art, those few 'visions of transcendence' which grace them: moments that Benjamin termed *Jetztzeiten.*[4]

---

[3] T.W. Adorno: *op. cit*, p.62.

[4] Richard Wolin: 'An Aesthetic of Redemption: Benjamin's Path to *Trauerspiel*', *Telos*, No. 43, Spring 1980, p. 72.

They hope to transpose musical works, as Benjamin did in relation to literary works, 'from the medium of the beautiful into that of truth — and thereby to *rescue and redeem*' such works. [5] And in so doing they hope to carry out the programme of the sociology of music, as Adorno saw it: namely, 'social critique accomplished through that of art'. [6]

To embark on a project of this kind is to engage in an attempt to construct a Marxist aesthetics of music — an endeavour as difficult as it is urgent. At a time when remarkable headway has been made in the development of Marxist aesthetics in other areas of artistic production (literature, painting and cinema, for example), one of the greatest obstacles in the way of the creation of a Marxist musical aesthetics is the obdurate hegemony of a bourgeois professional musical elite in all forums where 'classical' music is produced, taught, researched, theorized, or reproduced. So total is this hegemony that it is nearly impossible in the corridors of its influence to sustain the view that a different conceptualization of music could even be thought. A condition of one-dimensionality is here thoroughly installed: attempts to challenge and confront it produce a kind of scandal, if they are heard at all. But for all its great difficulties it is only through such confrontation — which cannot now be delayed any longer — that the possibility for a progressive cognition of music might be won. Though these essays are a virtual beginning in a global project that has hardly begun, they go forth in the hope that they might help to put the torch to that scandal.

CHRISTOPHER BALLANTINE

---

[5]   Jürgen Habermas: 'Consciousness-Raising or Redemptive Criticism — The Contemporaneity of Walter Benjamin', *New German Critique*, No. 17, Spring 1979, p.37.

[6]   T.W. Adorno: *op. cit.*, p.63.

Acknowledgements

Most of the essays in this book have appeared previously in various publications. 'Music and Society: the Forgotten Relationship', the text of my Inaugural Lecture given in the University of Natal, Durban, on October 9, 1974, was published by the University of Natal Press in 1974; 'Social and Philosophical Outlook in Mozart's Operas' appeared in *The Musical Quarterly*, Vol. 67, No. 4, October 1981; 'Beethoven, Hegel and Marx' appeared in *The Music Review*, Vol. 33, No. 1, February 1972; 'Charles Ives and the Meaning of Quotation in Music' appeared in *The Musical Quarterly*, Vol. 65, No. 2, April 1979; 'Towards an Aesthetic of Experimental Music', appeared in *The Musical Quarterly*, Vol. 63, No. 2, April 1977; and the three sections which constitute Chapter V ('Elite Music', 'Say it Straight' and 'Music to Forget') all appeared in *New Society*, in Vol. 14, November 13, 1969, in Vol. 15, June 4, 1970, and in Vol. 15, February 12, 1970, respectively. Acknowledgement is due to the editors and publishers involved for permission to reproduce these works. The essay on Sibelius was completed in 1971 and is published here for the first time.

Dr. Joseph Smith, the Gordon and Breach Musicology Series Editor, would expect his unobtrusive work to pass unnoticed and unmentioned, but I cannot miss this opportunity to express my real thanks for his unflagging editorial efficiency. His sharp editorial eye notwithstanding, the shortcomings of the book of course remain my own. Julie-Ann Mindry devised the index, and Richard Salmon re-drew the musical examples for Chapter VII.

The greatest debt is often mentioned last; and in my case it is a debt too substantial and too diverse to be mentioned in any detail. It is to Diana Simson: she alone will know the dimensions of my gratitude.

Chapter I

Music and Society:
The Forgotten Relationship

THE MUSICAL world that we so take for granted should today be a cause for grave concern rather than for the complacency that so typically attends it. The deformations that characterize the musical world at large are no less apparent in those havens of a supposedly purified and privileged musical practice: for instance the university or academy. To speak personally, my own deep disquiet about the nature of music and musical scholarship began about the time that I first entered the university musical world as an undergraduate. This disquiet has not mellowed with the passing of time. Today I am disturbed about how we see music and our relationship to it; about what we talk about when we discuss music, and those things that we somehow never find a place for in our discussions; about precisely what we teach and those things that we manage to leave out of our teaching, our researches and our scholarly writing. In a word, I am concerned about the highly selective nature of our preconceptions about music – all those notions that are part of our musical scenery and that we simply take for granted, and that therefore deeply influence the quality of our musical understanding. This is by no means a local problem: I think it occurs in most parts of the world with which we are familiar.

Let me begin by enunciating some of the simplest manifestations of the problem. One of the things that for most of us 'obvious', perhaps even 'natural', is that music is an art of

1

personal expression. We talk about a piece of music as expressing feelings, which have been put into it by the composer: we expect him to be somebody really out of the ordinary and certainly more than a mere craftsman. If he is great we say that he has genius. That means that he will be blessed with the gift of true originality: he will be a creator. His work will proceed less from calculation than from flashes of inspiration. To most of us, all this is so self-evident as to be trite. It is 'obvious'; it is 'true'. I am bound to point out that hardly any of this would be either obvious or true to anybody but ourselves: that for most of the time during the history of the West, and nearly all of the time in most other cultures, all of my definitions would have been rejected as utterly false and meaningless and would probably have led to my being regarded as something of a subversive. To take the example of the Middle Ages: music then was regarded as a mathematical discipline, and it very happily took its place alongside arithmetic, geometry, and astronomy as one of the four arts of the *quadrivium*. The different components of music – melody, harmony, rhythm – were hardly to be considered in terms of anything so human and subjective as inspiration: on the contrary, they were to be discussed in the precise terms of mathematical proportions. Cassiodorus, the great sixth-century writer on music, characteristically described music as *disciplina vel scientia quae de numeris loquitur:* the discipline or science that deals with numbers. And what about the composer as 'creative genius'? In the first place, the concept of genius as such did not exist. The composer was a craftsman, and his job was to follow the rules of his craft. Certainly, there was nothing special about him: he was seldom discussed in medieval writings, and hardly ever mentioned by name. Above all, he was *not* a creator. Medieval theology, which said that only God could create, made sure of that. A view that is surprising to us was perfectly obvious to people in the Middle Ages; and composers then showed their humble dependence on already created material by basing their new compositions on pre-existing ones.

Only when we approach the Renaissance do things begin to change; only then do we find the beginnings of the notion of genius, and a clear separation of craftsman and genius. The craftsman *reproduces,* in terms of the rules; the genius *transgresses,* in order to create. Simultaneously, we find the beginnings of the idea of music as a medium for expressing human emotions. What was formerly taboo now becomes not only permissible but even necessary, as society enters a new era with new potentialities and new demands: an order oriented towards man, discovery, individual achievement, great personalities and careers, and industrial and colonial conquest.

It will be evident that in my attempt to go beyond the 'obvious', I have had to look at more than the 'obvious' facts themselves: I have had to see these facts in their proper context, and only by exploring these relationships – and particularly those that reach down to the *social* situation — have I been able to understand the facts and see why something that is unthinkable at one time is perfectly obvious at another. Perhaps it will be said that by picking on such notions as genius, personal expression, and creativity I have picked on what might be termed a 'popular' confusion: no self-respecting music-lover or musical scholar or practitioner would make the sort of error I have talked about. If that is so, I would like to take the other extreme, and examine very briefly one of the most zealously cherished habits of university music departments: the cult of disinterested research. There is scarcely anything of which a musicologist is more proud than the methods and the achievements of historical musicology: no procedure in musical studies seems to him to be more obvious and correct, more independent of fluctuations in taste or outlook. For him, disinterested research – in the natural as well as the human sciences – came into being because we 'hit upon it': that is all. On closer inspection, however, the matter turns out to be rather more complex, and not quite so obvious. Modern scientific research came into being in the sixteenth and seventeenth centuries. But from the start a fierce theological and social battle was waged against it on many fronts. Science offended established interests: for this very reason science had of necessity to stress that research should be *disinterested.* So this criterion came to be built into its foundations, as it were, and precisely because of the social circumstances in the sixteenth and seventeenth centuries. The consequences of this were enormous. In particular, it came to be believed that all research and all knowledge were *valuable for their own sake,* and even more, that the *highest aim* of research was disinterested knowledge for its own sake. From this it followed that research which was undertaken for a practical end, such as the satisfaction of human needs, was regarded as being of a rather lower order. And so we have the situation today where vast quantities of research are done in the most obscure corners of countless fields – including music – with no particular purpose except the accumulation of still greater quantities of partial and atomized knowledge. One hardly needs to be reminded of how vigorously this state of affairs has been attacked in recent years.

I said I would begin by enunciating some of our simpler preconceptions – they might even be called prejudices – about music. In the process of doing that I have drawn the reader's attention to the necessity for us to think particularly about the social context if we wish to understand or see through these preconceptions. Now, the fact that I feel obliged to point this out and to argue that the method I have used is indispensable is itself a highly significant pointer to another of our preconceptions. This time it is a much more serious one: I would say even that it is fundamental.

Underlying nearly all our writing about music, all our talking about it and teaching of it, is the taken-for-granted assumption that music has very little to do with society; or alternatively, that if it is related somehow to society, the nature of this connection need not concern us very much, and that it is far more important to talk about styles, skills and techniques, and to keep to what we call the 'facts'. The orientations we are most used to, and that therefore seem to us perfectly natural and 'obvious', are invariably the ones we are least conscious of; and I admit that it was not until many years after I had begun to study music that I became aware of this particular orientation in our musical thinking. Once I noticed it, however, I saw it everywhere – in all our discussions about music at all levels, from the most erudite musicological treatise or scholarly textbook, to programme notes, casual conversations, and newspaper criticism. If I had not started to question this assumption, I would forever have regarded as 'obvious' that music is more or less abstract from life, that it develops in history pretty much according to its own immanent laws, or that the direction of its development is controlled 'from above' by composers of genius; I would forever have believed that music, being what we call an abstract art, is concerned aesthetically only with itself, and that its values are wholly internal to itself.

The truth of the matter, however, is very different. What actually happens is that social structures crystallize in musical structures; that in various ways and with varying degrees of critical awareness, the musical microcosm replicates the social macrocosm. For the moment a couple of very brief examples will have to suffice, though this is a point I will return to more than once. One can demonstrate, for instance, that the music of Bach is the way it is because Bach's music is appropriate to the *ancien régime;* and when the static Baroque style of Bach is replaced by the dynamic sonata style of Beethoven and others, this is wholly because of the collapse of late feudalism and its replacement by the bourgeois democratic order. To bring the whole argument up to date, one could make a similar analysis of contemporary popular music. The precise nature of 1960s rock music (for instance) is explicable *only* in relation to the protest and the possibilities for social change that were the lived experience of young people during that decade; the foreclosing of these possibilities and the shrinking of the horizons of change that characterize the 1970s determine the altered structures of the typical popular music of the 1970s: on the one hand the total sell-out of disco music, on the other the brittle and authentic criticism of the repressive social order so well articulated by punk rock.

So the assumption that music and society are wholly separate domains is demonstrably false. I began to question such assumptions at the moment that I began to suspect them to be rationalizations. As I investigated, it struck me that such atomistic views had not always been held – in fact, they were of quite recent origin. And I saw that they came into being when and where they did – in the industrial capitalist countries in the late nineteenth century – because the bourgeoisie then *needed* to hold such views, even though they ran contrary to what had been believed up to half a century earlier. Exactly why this was can here be stated only very briefly.

The French Revolution had promised a better future for all human beings. If that future was to indefinitely postponed – and the entrenchment of the bourgeoisie during the nineteenth century made that inevitable – then all forms of bourgeois thought, including aesthetics, would need to show a similar turning away from the great problems of the age, a similar flight from reality and a movement towards abstraction. The connection, then, between Europe in the age of imperialism and an aesthetician such as Worringer with his 'theory of abstraction' and his rejection of realism, is not in the least fortuitous.

For this way of viewing the matter, I am indebted to the Marxist tradition. Since this is not primarily an essay on Marxist epistemology, I cannot now give a full theoretical account of precisely how one must proceed if one wishes to de-hoax social phenomena so that the real web of interrelations, as well as the deceits and rationalizations, is revealed. I want simply to say that as a practising musician I find this kind of insight indispensable to my practical and theoretical involvement with music every day at every level. For critical social theorists have shown us that very often the views people have of themselves, their world, and their place in it, are far removed from what is actually and demonstrably the case. As Marx pointed out, it is true of social groups just as it is true of individuals, that if you want to form an opinion of someone you do not go about it merely by asking him his own opinion of himself. Now if this is the case, we can hardly claim that our views about music are exempt from these limitations. Our attitudes to music, the categories we impose on it, the analytical structures we bring to bear upon it, the way we explain it – all these are subject to the same laws: they too are a complex mixture of truths, half-truths, confusions and total falsehood.

The reality we have to come to terms with is that our 'un-reflected-upon' attitudes to music – those attitudes that we take for granted, and that seem to us most obvious, with all their implicit assumptions – are very largely *ideology*. That is to say, they have come into being at a specific moment in history, as part and parcel of the way certain classes of people have come to see their world and their place and activities in it, all of which have been more or less a function of the way society has been organized at that time, and particularly of the way it has shared, or rather denied the sharing of, its benefits. Such views are the products of certain societies in certain social and historical conditions, and of the individuals in them: people who by virtue of their place in the social structure are to greater or lesser degree cut off from seeing it *as a whole*, as it really is. Ideology, then, in this sense is a kind of false consciousness.

This has a very special, and uniquely troubling, significance for us today. As many social philosophers have pointed out, it is today quite remarkably difficult for ordinary men and women to *see* the whole, to grasp the social reality behind the ideological veil. In some respects it is more difficult now than it has been at any time in the last hundred years. This is partly, but not only, because of the increasing complexity of Western societies; there are in addition at least four further interrelated reasons for this predicament. Firstly, there is the continuing contraction of human consciousness through the increasingly specialized nature of disciplines and occupations. One of the most disastrous products of this tendency is the person who is at one and the same time illiterate and a graduate of a university. 'This is a man' comments the French-speaking Marxist philosopher Goldmann, 'who is very familiar with one field of production and has high professional qualifications to carry out in a satisfactory and even remarkable manner the tasks which are assigned to him, but who is increasingly losing all contact with the rest of human life, and whose personality is thus being deformed and narrowed to an extreme degree'.[1] Secondly, there is the steady erosion – and even total dis-appearance – of responsibility in social life. One of the differences, for the middle-class person, between the so-called liberal capitalism of one-hundred years ago and the centralized mass-production society of today, is that he finds fewer and fewer areas where he can act in a way that makes any difference, or can hold views that will *matter*. The real decisions are always taken *elsewhere:* he merely carries them out. Thirdly – and this is the payoff – because Western societies offer increasing material rewards, they also seem to offer their own self-justification. The fetishization of consumer goods stifles criticism before it can even be formulated. And fourthly, because of the centralization, the all-pervasiveness, and the insidiously sophisticated techniques of the communications industry, the consciousness of people today is dominated and administered to an alarming extent.

The picture is bleak; but the implication, I think, is clear. It is that today – as a matter of urgency – one of our very few lifelines is to use every resource at our command to be on our guard against the disfigured consciousness that I have described as ideology. We have to be exceedingly vigilant about not submitting passively to what seems most 'obvious'; we have vigorously to question the values, the categories, the responses, that we unconsciously pick up – no matter whether these concern life, or politics, or art in general, or (and this is what I am preoccupied with here) music. Only through a special kind of effort, and a profound concern, not for the immediate and superficial rewards offered by the present order, but for the real interests of humanity in the long term and on the broadest conceivable base: only in this way will we be able to make a start at comprehending the *whole,* and clearing our minds and senses of the encrustations of ideology. But it will only be a start; serious moral concern is not in itself enough. What I mean by this I shall attempt to make clear later on.

I must now say that I think that our task as musicians and music-lovers is today complicated in still another dimension, which I have so far not touched on. This only increases my concern that I spoke of at the beginning, and convinces me that the sort of criticisms I am making of the quality of our musical understanding are now more urgently necessary than they have ever been. This further complication (it is a horrifying one,

Good Opening

though I think the other arts are affected in an almost identical way) is that music today has itself entered into partnership with ideology. Mass produced, and turned into a commodity like everything else, music now serves a very special function: it is the perfumed balm to tranquillize and lubricate a system geared to profits. In this gutted and predigested form we meet music everywhere: it is the gentle ooze that welcomes us in supermarkets, anaesthetizes frayed nerves in offices and factories, exhales over us in lifts and aeroplanes, screams at us from ice-cream vans, sings radio and TV commercials at us with mind-deadening regularity and leaves us humming to the tune of Coca-Cola, American cigarettes and beauty soap. And although this applies most obviously to what we call 'popular' musical styles, there is hardly a sphere of contemporary music or of the 'classical' music of the past that is immune to this sort of expropriation. When Beethoven's Fifth Symphony accompanies a summons to buy this or that brand of washing powder; when Mozart's G minor symphony is tarted up and truncated into a three-minute marketable commodity that can be heard fifteen times a day, every day; when Bach booms from the transistor radio to add to the noise of the floor polisher, and Berlioz introduces the latest Stock Exchange report: then it is questionable whether we can ever really *hear* Beethoven, Mozart, Bach or Berlioz again. What such associations, and such listening habits, actually do to our ability to *hear* – by which, as a musician, I must mean our ability to be quickened and enlightened by a profound musical utterance – is something we have scarcely begun to consider. Nor, I fear, is it something we worry very much about. We take it for granted, along with so much else. And anyway, it is part and parcel of our way of life and our standard of living, and that, we are told, is getting better all the time. So, in the words of a well-known song of the communications industry, why worry? The line of thought is impenetrably circular.

But that is only part of what I mean by saying that music has become entangled with ideology. I also mean something else. For the last century-and-a-half, virtually ever since Beethoven, it has been getting more and more difficult for composers –

even the most serious composers – to write music that is both very good and very popular. This seems somewhat paradoxical, since it was, of course, precisely during the last century-and-a-half that audiences for 'classical' music grew so tremendously. But I think these two things are linked, and that therefore the paradox is a necessary one. What undoubtedly happened during the last one-and-a-half centuries was that the demands of good or great music, and the demands of popular music, tended to pull in diametrically opposite directions, so that it was progressively more difficult to write good music if one wanted also to be popular, or to write popular music if one wanted to be great. And notice that I said progressively more difficult: I do not want to deny that there were some composers who managed, at times, to come close to both greatness and popularity. The reason for this difficulty, I want to suggest, is that music – indeed the very language of 'classical' music itself – fell victim to commercialization. In the capitalist economy, where the individual who did best was the one who geared himself most ruthlessly to the biggest turnover, and where the composer like everybody else had to come to terms with this principle or perish, the composer who did 'best' (in financial terms) was the one who had his eye most firmly on the box office. But the box office of course has no standards, except quantitative ones. And so the language of Western 'classical' music by turns adapted itself to the box office – not only in the work of composers whose names we have forgotten, but also to a marked degree in the music of many well-known and serious composers. Think for example of late nineteenth century piano music, to mention just one area. However fine much of this music is, and whatever its positive contributions to musical and pianistic technique, it remains nevertheless true that one often wants to apply to it such epithets as 'cheap', 'showy', 'superficial', 'slushy'. One frequently wants to say that it strives for a sort of brilliant glitter for its own sake, that is strives for immediate effect, that is tries to ingratiate itself. It hardly needs pointing out that these are the very same terms some of us would use to describe many of the consumer goods that we are asked to buy every day of our lives. (Much music has unknowingly taken on the very character of a society it should be helping us to become critically aware of: much music blindly reproduces the values of the established way of life, instead of refusing these values. It is her also that I see music entangled with ideology.)

This kind of corruption of language, as I have hinted, is by no means peculiar to music: it afflicts the other arts as well. John Berger, for example, has incisively documented the assimilation of painting to property;[2] and Richard Hoggart, while Professor of English in the University of Birmingham, wrote as follows about the problems of writing in the English language today:

> I wonder whether in any previous period so many words were being used, as we might say, *inorganically* – not because the writers had something to say about their experience, *but on behalf of the particular concerns of others;* when so much language was used not as exploration but as persuasion and manipulation; when so much prose had its eye only slightly on the object and almost wholly on the audience, when so many words proclaimed, if you listened to them carefully within their contexts, not 'I touch and illuminate experience' but 'this will roll them in the aisles'.
>
> More important: in such circumstances it becomes more difficult to write *decently* about any thoughts and feelings. It would be very easy to compile a black list of words which are not usable until they have been redefined by each writer within each particular context. Not the old words we are all used to laughing about – 'tragedy' for the popular press, or 'magnificent' for Metro-Goldwyn-Mayer. The process goes on quickly and becomes more sophisticated all the time. The newer men have quieter voices. So words like 'sincere', 'creative', 'vital', 'homely' and 'love' go out of decent use. . . . . That is why, we say, a writer finds his tools going blunt in his hands.[3]

The French structuralist Barthes has written rather more cryptically about the same issue. 'In the present state of history', he says, 'all political writing can only confirm a police-universe, just as all intellectual writing can only produce a para-literature which does not dare any longer to tell its name.'

I have said that one of the most serious and fundamental of our taken-for-granted assumptions – serious and fundamental not only because it is heinous and unscholarly in itself, but also because it blinds us to the falsehood of many of our other assumptions – is the belief that the connection between music and society, if we ever concede that such a connection exists at all, can safely be ignored or dismissed in a few vague platitudes about the *Zeitgeist*. We ought to remind ourselves that it was not always so. Until relatively recent times, composers, performers, theorists, were a highly unified and integrated group: the boundaries between who composed, who performed and who theorized were hardly significant. Much the same was true of the other arts, for example, literature. And as happened also in those other arts, such people saw music as immersed in life: not only deriving from society, but returning to it and affecting the quality of life in a most profound way. These were people who had universal and inseparable social, artistic, human and political interests. Such concerns formed a dynamic unified system; they had not yet split off and hardened into narrow, specialized disciplines. We tend too easily to forget that this atomization of perspective is neither natural nor given: it is something we have brought about, and it fundamentally distinguishes the modern period from the Renaissance, the Enlightenment, and indeed all eras up to the so-called heroic period of the bourgeoisie. Literature, by virtue of its explicitness, provides a particularly vivid insight into the kind of universality that characterized artistic endeavour in the days before such activity fragmented into specialized fields. *Hamlet* is only the most famous example of a literary work that includes within itself a substantial and representative discourse on the relationship of art to reality; other examples are to be found throughout literature, from Aristophanes to Goethe and Balzac. All the most influential philosophers of art stressed this relationship: Aristotle and Hegel, for instance, methodically developed the idea that art existed in a systematic relationship with reality; and Hegel showed that the ascent and decline of artistic forms could be understood only as arising from the socio-historical evolution of mankind. Indeed, the significance of such philosophers for the theory of art derives precisely from the fact that they were important social theoreticians as well as aestheticians. Now in historical practice, this whole line of thought has been carried to a logical and radical conclusion.

Great artists in every field have based their work on the presumption that by working in and on the present, they could contribute to the realization of a better future. Schiller, for example, said that the political problem of a better society 'must take the path through the aesthetic realm, because it is through beauty that one arrives at freedom'. In his poem, *The Artists*, he wrote:

> What we have here percceived as beauty,
> We shall someday encounter as truth.

Balzac saw his task in even more active and concrete terms. 'What Napoleon began with the sword', he said, 'I shall complete with the pen.' And in similar vein, listen to Handel. After a performance of the *Messiah*, an aristocratic admirer thanked Handel for the 'noble entertainment' which he had recently given the town. 'My Lord', replied Handel, 'I should be sorry if I only entertained them; *I wish to make them better*'.

These are some of the things that by and large we in the musical world do not talk about today, or worry about. Or if ever we do talk about them, too often we do so with the uncomfortable sense that what we are doing is not quite legitimate. Our universe of discourse is circumscribed by technical matters. We talk about wrong notes in performance, criticize parallel fifths in a student's harmony exercise, discriminate between different musical styles, analyze the formal and technical aspects of a musical work, comment on the relationship between two conflicting editions of the same work, and so on. I do not want to deny that each of these things may, in its proper place, be valid and important; but I am worried that such concerns are for the most part *all* we talk about. The consequence of this, it seems to me, is that in most parts of the world at the present time musicians have very little of interest to say about their own art. I search each month with growing fatigue through the musical and musicological journals, the newly published books, the lists of forthcoming publications – including abstracts of such works in many

B

languages – in a quest for evidence of any attempts to see music in relation to the larger social contexts I have been discussing, and thereby to account objectively and concretely for the specifics of the musical culture of which we are a part. I find this monthly search a most depressing undertaking. Our approach to musical history, for instance, seems to be about on a par with the level of development of general academic history in the nineteenth century – and that, as Eric Hobsbawm has pointed out, was 'an extremely, one might almost say deliberately, backward discipline'.[4] The music historian's job, we think, following Leopold von Ranke, is 'simply to show how it really was' – in other words, to get to the facts. The facts of music history, we assume, are like the facts of natural science: isolated, there for the taking, and discoverable by means of philology, textual criticism and archaeological spade-work. Such an attitude, although it has undeniably given us a number of empirical techniques for verifying certain types of documentary evidence, is premissed upon an old, naive, positivistic view of history. The British historian, Gareth Stedman Jones, has spelt out the implications of such a view, and pointed to its fundamental error. According to this view, he writes,

history was an objective thing. It was physically recorded in myriad bundles of archives from the Public Record Office to the local parish church. The task of the historian was to write it up. Theory would come, like steam from a kettle when it reached boiling point. The initial illusion is evident. Those who tried to create theory out of facts, never understood that it was only theory that could constitute them as facts in the first place. Similarly those who focused history upon the event, failed to realize that events are only meaningful in terms of a structure which will establish them as such.[5]

I have been sketching a picture of contemporary musical studies, of popular attitudes to music, and of music itself, and have argued that all of these are subject to ideological distortions of various kinds. I have tried to suggest that these distortions consist in our habit of seeing music in an atomized way, as so many facts and techniques, cut off from a fundamental structural intimacy with its social order. Now in opposition to this somewhat dismal state of affairs a few voices have been raised: they are, I am afraid, lone voices, and they are heard but rarely, and hardly ever at any length. Yet what is significant is that they are the voices of some of the most eminent musical thinkers of our time. Though I would not presume that all of these scholars would agree either with everything I have said, or with each other, they are nevertheless clearly very worried about many of these same basic issues. I do not care much for catalogues, but since the views of these scholars lend weight to my own, I should like very briefly to recount a few of them.

The German musical scholar Georg Knepler argues that perhaps there is no such thing as 'music history'. 'When we deal with our subject', he says, 'we are, whether we know it or not, concerned with the history of man.' In making a plea for the history, sociology, psychology, analysis, and aesthetics of music (and other disciplines) 'to ask one another more exact questions', he is insisting that what we do *not* need is still more blind piling up of data, uninformed by theory. 'We have a store of knowledge and we don't know what to do with it', he says. 'The *theory* of historiography and the *theory* of musicology are much less developed than the accumulation of even more knowledge. . . I only wish to emphasize how important it is to take a more universal view of all facets of our discipline'.[6] F.L. Harrison, the English scholar, evidently concurs. For him, the aim of the academic study of music is the study of men in society, through the music they use. This means, incidentally, that one has no right to ignore popular music. Harrison maintains that 'it is the function of all musicology to be in fact ethnomusicology, that is, to take its range of research to include material that is termed "sociological".' Thus musicology should have what he calls a 'social aim': namely, to enlarge man's knowledge of himself and of his social development.[7] In Yugoslavia, Ivo Supičič approvingly quotes Robert Erich Wolf's criticism of the usual narrow academic approach to music;[8] the criticism goes as follows:

... well furnished as it is with knowledge and techniques of the past, musicology still largely ignores past attitudes, the psycho-philosophical climate which made use of those techniques for an aesthetic end. Neither literary nor art historians are so indifferent to this significant tool; musicologists lag far behind their colleagues in parallel disciplines, and while the latter have . . . the advantage of dealing with – apparently – more 'concrete' materials, musicologists need not abandon the quest because of the more 'abstract' nature of their art.[9]

A similar fresh wind blows from several places in America. If we study music in order to study man in society, then we ought to guard against being too ethnocentric. Mantle Hood reminds us that art history and criticism are based on the assumption of a world of art. He goes on:

Music history and criticism have remained insular in their promulgation of Western theories and tradition. Any kind of insularity is hardly compatible with the demands of the last half of the twentieth century.[10]

For Edward A. Lippman, the problem is that musical research is 'too positivistic, too preoccupied with the collection of data and the determination of detail'.[11] Gilbert Chase would agree; we have reached an impasse, and the major breakthrough, he believes,

will occur only through the fusion of the two disciplines – historical musicology and ethnomusicology – under the more impelling impact of the social sciences, to which we must necessarily look for an understanding of the forces that are even now changing the shape of society in the post-industrial era.[12]

This would seem to imply that some sort of synthesis, and the formulation of adequate theoretical methods, is necessary if our musical understanding is to develop; and these, significantly, are precisely the terms of Charles Seeger's criticism. Seeger writes:

In comparison with the most admired scholarly disciplines of the twentieth-century Western World, musicology has only tardily formed concepts of its total field, or universe, and of its lowest common denominator. And these concepts, such as they are, have not yet made a dent upon the 'excessive historicism' still entrenched in academic fortresses. Meanwhile, the natural and social sciences have advanced from positions of main reliance upon analytical techniques to bold syntheses of universal proportions, while in musicology, even mention of synthesis is not quite respectable.[13]

Implicit in many of these writings is one further theme, and one that I have harped on throughout this essay. It is that if we see music in isolation from society, we shall not only distort its meaning, but what we say will be subject to serious factual error. Paul Henry Lang, doyen of American musicologists, bolsters his attack with an example of such an error. He observes that,

the Baroque started out as an expression of the *Ecclesia militans*, of the Counter Reformation, but as it spread from the Latin-Catholic south to the German-Protestant north the original motive gave way to a different set of ideas. Yet musicology persists in dealing with Baroque music in elaborate isolation, expecting to explain it by purely stylistic research and elucidation, but producing only a good picture of formal and technical developments without accounting for the underlying meaning... [The researchers,] by restricting themselves to chronology, paleography, morphology, typology, and general *Fachlehre*, ... lost sight of the idea and missed its mutation.[14]

All these writings are raids on the 'obvious', as transmitted from teacher to pupil in music-teaching institutions in most parts of the world. As such, they may seem rather academic and a little remote from the immediate concerns of anybody not actually involved in the business of teaching, or studying, music. This is not the conclusion I should like to be drawn. As I have implied from the outset, if our attitudes to music urgently need spring-cleaning, up-dating, rebuilding, and a number of other even more radical operations, it is not only in university music departments that such revisions have to be made but everywhere music of any description is played, talked about, talked over, bought, sold, ignored, or sensitively listened to. This, of course, is not to deny that music departments may have a special responsibility for reducing the amount of noxious academic dust that is produced in lecture rooms and libraries, inhaled by students, and exhaled for years to come in classrooms, concert halls, homes, and the columns of the daily press. If this suggests the idea of a sort of academic pollution, I do not think the image will be gratuitous. The situation is, after all, rather a desperate one. Lang – to quote him again – speaks of the 'pitiful state of our popular literature on music' and laments the total non-existence of 'an intelligent reading public comparable to that interested in the visual arts'; the blame for both, he believes, rests with the music-teaching institutions. He argues that musical education at university level is by and large 'not an integral part of what is considered a "liberal" education; it does not aim at training the intellect, and bears little resemblance to the studies pursued in the other humanistic disciplines'. He points to the existence of 'a marked gulf between cultural patterns prevailing in the other divisions of the university's school of arts and letters, and the music department'.[15] This undoubtedly has some bearing on what F.L. Harrison means in his apocalyptic statement that 'there appears to be a near-breakdown of the dissemination of knowledge of one of the central arts of Western society'.[16] I do not know whether it is more shocking to register such serious criticisms, or to admit that they are almost never made.

At this stage we should not lose sight of what I, and the scholars I have quoted, see as being basic to this shrivelling and ossification of the musical mentality of our culture: namely, the shrinking of the legitimate area for musical pursuits to a narrow field of technical and 'factual' matters, a field that excludes the plenitude of music's extra-musical relationships and, most disastrously of all, excludes the social and human context that gives music its meaning. Before I attempt to suggest how we might go about liberating our minds from this predicament, I should like to point out what I think is a rather nice contradiction between the way we think and the way we act in this regard. If a sense of the essential relationship between music and society has dropped out of our consciousness, then it may surprise us to discover that our musical behaviour belies our avowed theory and confirms the very truth of this music-society relationship. I think this can be shown very quickly. It is often lamented that we *really* like only the music of the period from Bach to World War I, at the outer limits. Usually, it's assumed that this is so *merely* because we are not sufficiently exposed to earlier, or more recent, music. Doubtless this is true to a degree. But it seems to me that there is a much more fundamental reason why we love the music of this historical period above all others. It is that this music speaks to us of the life-style we are so busy living and so earnestly involved in trying to preserve. To put it rather bluntly, as members of the bourgeoisie we like affirmative bourgeois music. From this it follows, of course, that we could discover a great deal about ourselves if we learnt to 'read the character' of this music – an enterprise that presupposes, but goes beyond, mere technical analysis. My own methodical attempts at this kind of musical 'character analysis' have convinced me that, paradoxically, we applaud in such music not only values which coincide with the way we live, but also values that run quite opposite to it. When we speak about 'the great composers' as being those who were most *creative* and most *original,* we are applauding precisely the kind of achievements that have opened the options for human progress and freedom in the bourgeois era – even though in discussing such composers we may think we are talking *only* about technical categories. Conversely, part of our admiration for 'the great composers' depends upon their music transcending – even negating – the present order. My own work on Beethoven,[17] for example, has shown that Beethoven remains one of our very greatest composers because his music *enacts* the most radical ideals of the French Revolution, which appeal to us precisely to the extent that a happy and liberated life for all human beings has *not* been realized in the present social order. It would be perfectly legitimate to ask why we cherish some values in music that we are content to see trodden underfoot in society. One might want to answer by saying that we applaud such values in art because there they are relegated to the category of idealistic fantasy. This argument has the familiar ring: 'It would be nice if. . .; but human nature being what it is. . .,' etc. But this is not good enough. The *reverence* with which we treat music, and all art, defies our relegating it to the category of make-believe: I think we have to say that music embodies aspirations which are the real aspirations of all of us *in spite of ourselves.* Marcuse, in 1937, coined a memorable term for these aspirations in art: he called them 'a remembrance of what could be'. 'Only in art', he went on to say, 'has bourgeois society tolerated its own ideals and taken them seriously.'[18]

This has been in the way of a short digression, but I hope it has helped to make my earlier point: namely, that although we forget that a profound relationship exists between music and society, our musical behaviour nevertheless confirms that relationship. Our actions belie our beliefs. But the corollary is also true: our beliefs are far from being able to comprehend or explain our practice – and especially those aspects of our practice that reflect most deeply on our intimate musical preferences. Given these beliefs, we cannot account for our deepest likes and dislikes. Mere technical analysis of the musical work, incidentally, cannot do this for us either – as the most honest and intelligent technical analysts freely admit. A leading American musical analyst, Edward T. Cone, for example, has written that 'it would be tempting to state that analysis can demonstrate the quality of the work'; there is, however,[19] 'a final step that is completely beyond the confines of analysis'.

I have taken a considerable but, I think, a necessary length of time to arrive at the crucial question that I wish now to formulate. It is this. If our taken-for-granted assumptions about music lead us so promptly into the dead-ends of ideology, factual error, false hypothesis, self-contradiction, helplessness before the facts, and a rampant popular ignorance about music, what are we to do about it? How are we to escape from these crippling limitations? How do we evolve a theory that comprehends our practice, and how do we become critically sensitive to the distorting ideology that is built into our musical consciousness, institutions, textbooks, and mass media? In proposing an answer, I want to be a bit more systematic than my colleagues, those lone voices whom I quoted earlier. I believe that the answer—to put it in rather philosophical language—is to recover the category of the dynamic totality; that is to say, to grasp the concept of the *whole* (understood as being in a process of change) and to situate it at the centre of all our discussions, all our thinking and doing in regard to our art. This is a very difficult matter and we shall not achieve it overnight. But before we can even begin, we shall of course need to know what it is that I am talking about. What then is this category of the totality?

Very briefly, it is a view of human activity as something which belongs to a greater whole, which extends both spatially and in time and which thus embraces the totality of our social, physical, economic, historical, and cultural world. It is an insistence, therefore, that no part of our activity can be understood by wrenching it out of the whole that gives it its meaning, and trying to understand it in isolation. The part belongs inseparably to the whole: to understand either the part, or the whole, one has therefore to meet two essential conditions: one has to consider both the part and the whole together; and one has to realize that these are not *static* entities, but rather aspects of a social system in a process of *historical change*. It is impossible to divorce the spiritual side of life – including music and the arts – from the material side, or to divorce either of these from their history. If one wishes to acquire a scientific understanding of social life, this bi-focal – or rather multi-focal – view is the only way to do it. The method which Descartes urged, namely, 'to divide each of the difficulties ... into as many parts as possible, as might be required for an easier solution', may be valid to a degree in the natural sciences, but in the human sciences it is almost completely useless. In the human sciences one has to be what is sometimes called 'dialectical'. This is obviously not the place to go fully into the pros and cons of the dialectical method: I want now merely to assert this as an approach I believe we in the arts ought to take very seriously indeed. *How* correct and *how* important it is, is a question that has been answered by, among others, the important twentieth-century thinker, Lucien Goldmann. To ask, he says,

whether the social sciences ought to be dialectical or not means purely and simply to ask if they ought to understand reality or to distort and obscure it: in spite of its different and, *apparently even contrary*, aspect, it is the same battle which, in the seventeenth century, the physicists fought against the particular interests of forces bound to the past and to the Church, the struggle against particular ideologies for a free, objective and human knowledge.[20]

The point I want to stress is that we need this dynamic, and ultimately critical, concept of the whole in order to save ourselves from the related scourges of error, ignorance, and ideology. Honest immediacy and innocent intuition are not enough; all the faith and goodwill in the world are insufficient to provide an objective basis for reflection about music. In a splintered and reified world where the real relationships that constitute the whole are not immediately apparent, theory alone can reveal these connections, including those that bear upon music. I have already mentioned the view, held by many radical thinkers, that today the basic truths about our society and the way we live are remarkably inaccessible to ordinary consciousness; and I have suggested that neither music nor our attitude to it can automatically be exempt from the resultant 'false consciousness'. What all this means is that today musical discussions of any kind will tend to get hopelessly lost if the talk is *only* about music: composers will get lost if they talk only about composing, sponsors only about sponsoring, musicologists only about musicology, music teachers only about music teaching, and so on. All of these must orient themselves towards the concept of the dynamic totality, which is the one procedure that has even the possibility of guaranteeing that these become critically aware not only of themselves, their goals, methods, and techniques, but also of the social and historical reality within which they operate. I have no wish to pretend that this is not very difficult; or to pretend that the odds are not loaded against it by the entire present structure of our musical life. But before we throw up our hands in despair, let us take note of the fact that great advances have been made in the other arts, and even, in one virtually unique instance, in music itself – in the work of T.W. Adorno.

Since, however, such developments have met with much more general approval in the other arts than in music, I should like very briefly to mention a few of the significant features of these other achievements. Ever since the early years of the century art historians have been learning that the great works of painting and sculpture, and the stylistic and technical changes in art, can be properly understood and assessed only in relation to the social totality of which they are a part. One of the starting-points of this development was the year 1904 when a scholar in Vienna noted that nobody had been able to explain the sudden emergence of the art of the Van Eycks, and went on to show that the wellsprings of their art could only be found in – of all places! – books of economic history. Since then the achievements of art history – including the correcting of errors – have been impressive. Art historians have discovered, for example, that a purely formalistic approach to medieval architecture obscures precisely what was most important to medieval men and women: namely, the *content* of the architecture, its religious implications. They have discovered that because (say) Romanesque art, or the art of the Italian Renaissance, is so deeply rooted in the social and political conditions of its time, it is a falsification of the style to treat it in isolation from such conditions. In a discussion of some of the achievements of this method – which has very largely changed the character of art history – Frederick Antal has pointed out that such art historians have also learnt one other vital lesson: namely, that 'there is no contradiction between a picture as a work of art and as a document of its time, since the two are complementary'.[21]

But probably the greatest strides of all have been made in the field of literature – and there largely as a result of the lifelong efforts of Georg Lukács, the great Hungarian literary critic, philosopher, and sociologist. It seems to me quite evident that serious musical studies will make no further significant advance until they have, *as a first step,* assimilated the work of a thinker such as Lukács, and that of his school. Needless to say, it will not be a simple matter of taking over and then mechanically applying the concepts which Lukács has worked out with such astonishing rigour, profundity and subtlety in relation to the literary work of art. All of these concepts, although some may *appear* to turn upon purely literary

questions, have, in Lukács's formulations, an inescapable
relation to the totality, to the social and historical whole within
which the work of art comes to life. But because of obvious and
fundamental differences between music and literature, we shall
need to do a lot of work on these concepts before we know how –
or even if – we can apply them to music, or whether, guided by
Lukács's *concerns,* we need to look for different concepts which
may be more fitting to the musical work of art.

An example might help to illustrate what I mean. One of
Lukács's key categories is the concept of realism. This idea is
inseparable from the view that I have already touched on, that
the way the world immediately appears to be, is not the way it
'really' is. Its surface appearances are mystifying: they are
rationalizations that hide from view the dynamics that actually
govern the social world. Lukács himself summarizes this view
by availing himself of a famous quotation: 'Science', he recalls
Marx as saying, 'would be superfluous if there were an immediate coincidence of the appearance and reality of things'. Now
realism in art exists precisely in order to bridge this gulf
between the way things seem to be and the way they truly are.
Lukács puts it as follows:

> The goal for all great art is to provide a picture of reality in which the
> contradiction between appearance and reality, the particular and the general,
> the immediate and the conceptual, etc., is so resolved that the two converge
> into a spontaneous integrity in the direct impression of the work of art and
> provide a sense of an inseparable integrity. The universal appears as a quality
> of the individual and the particular, reality becomes manifest and can be
> experienced within appearance, the general principle is exposed as the
> specific impelling cause for the individual case being specifically depicted.[22]

Lukács, explains that *how* this contradiction of appearance
and reality is overcome in art is the achievement of *form.* Form,
he says, raises content to objectivity in art; it is 'a specific mode
of reflection of reality'; it is 'the shortest way to the top'. In art,
content must *become* form; and in the same way, form must
become content. The unity of form and content *makes possible*
the unity of appearance and reality, of the particular and the

universal, of the individual and the typical. And with this theory, Lukács can quite easily account for the *effect* of the work of art. The effect of art, he says,

results from the fact that the work by its very nature offers a truer, more complete, more vivid and more dynamic reflection of reality than the recipient otherwise possesses, that it conducts him. . . beyond the bounds of his experiences toward a more concrete insight into reality.[23]

The obvious question is, of course: How could we apply some of these concepts to music? Is there any musical equivalent for realism – for discovering the reality behind the appearance, and making it manifest *in* the appearance? What, if anything, is the musical equivalent of objectivity? I don't think these questions are as unanswerable as they may at first seem. It seems likely that we can say something about the 'content' of various musical genres. Sonata would seem to have duality or even conflict – of keys, themes and so on – as one of its primary contents. The content of a Gothic motet might possibly be the harmonious accord into which the brilliant scholastic mind can bring the most diverse and independent components – notably, characteristic melodies and texts from opposing sacred and secular realms. Another aspect of the content of a musical work is surely the logic and the principles according to which it operates. What, in other words, are its own internal laws? These laws change in music from time to time – in fact, they change constantly. For instance, at a certain time in history equality and unity of the simultaneous lines in a musical work is expected; at another time it is not: thus the great age of polyphony gives way to a more homophonic period. In the Baroque, music moves by a process of, so to speak, unravelling its *given* implications; in the Classical era, a piece of music leads itself beyond the given, and so discovers the unexpected. Once we have conceptualized such laws, or such contents, we can then ask to what extent they are objective, in Lukács's sense. How far do they succeed in giving us an auditory image of the real, objective dynamics of their own particular historical age? Or, to use different words, how far do these musical laws reflect the real inherent laws of their social contexts? And – just as important – how far are these laws realized in a form that allows them adequate expression? When we have answered such questions, incidentally, we shall also be in a position to see music as a way of *knowing*, and shall therefore be able to judge objectively whether a given piece is 'true' or 'false'.

Lukács's work – in its entirety undoubtedly one of the greatest intellectual achievements of the last hundred years – is full of formulations whose possible application to music needs urgently to be explored. Another of these, closely related to those I have already mentioned, is his outline of a theory of genres. In discussing a genre, one is discussing a specific and concrete relationship between form, content, and theme. Lukács explains that an artist can of course treat his subject matter in any way he wishes – but not all treatments will be equally successful. He gives the example of Zola trying to extend a short story by Balzac into a full-length novel: Zola's novel failed where Balzac's story on the same subject succeeded, not because Balzac was talented and Zola was not, but because with Balzac 'the short-story form grows out of the essential quality of the theme and subject matter'. Zola *could* have written a novel on Balzac's theme – the tragic plight of the modern artist – but to do so he would have had to find 'entirely different subject matter and an entirely different plot'. When we obtain a theory of genres, says Lukács, 'we will then be able to see that every genre has its own specific objective laws which no artist can ignore without peril'.[24]

All these notions – appearance and reality, objectivity in art, form and content, the theory of genres – are intrinsically interrelated: not because Lukács wishes them to be, but because they too are aspects of the whole, the totality that encompasses each individual in all his material and spiritual relations. They are therefore an essential aspect of human history as well, and they change – both in themselves and in relation to each other – as and when our history changes. A number of profound and simple truths emerge from this realization, with obvious significance for music. There can, for example, be no such thing as a musical form to suit all of history's occasions: musical forms are justified by history, not by composers, and still less by writers of textbooks. Even more dramatic is the logical inference that therefore no composer – no artist in any sphere – if he wishes to produce art of relevance and integrity, is free to do just as he pleases. For art to be seen to be great, it must also be seen to be necessary.

I have discussed Lukács because he seems to me to be one of the most important and influential of those thinkers about art who deal with what I have called the category of the dynamic totality. Moreover, because of the clarity, cogency and number of his theoretical concepts, he is one of the thinkers in this tradition whose work is most suggestive to musicians. But there are many other writers in this tradition, at least one of whom, Theodor Adorno, I particularly regret not having had space to discuss. In recommending the work of these thinkers as correct in method, I do not want it to be thought that I am claiming infallibility for them. What I am arguing is that they have brought into being a mode of discourse that posits the notion of a *dynamic, dialectical whole,* and thus certainly meets the first prerequisite of making explicit once again that unity between art and society that was so fundamental to all artistic activity before the bourgeois era.

Only within the perspective of such a method shall we begin to be fully conscious of, for example, the choices, evaluations, and discriminations that we make about music, and objectively of why we make them; only then can we intervene in these choices, and where necessary rescue them from ideology. At the moment, most of the discussions we have about music are abstract, because they fail to recognize that the question – both now and in the past – about what kind of *music* we want is dependent upon the prior question about what kind of *world* we want. Our need today is to see that most of our agreements and disagreements about 'good' or 'bad' music are, in fact, disputes *not* (as we suppose) about 'aesthetic value' as some mystical or abstract category, a self-enclosed system remote from the concerns of ordinary life, and with terms that have meaning and reference only within the system. On the contrary, we need to understand that these agreements or dis-agreements revolve around values that we hold to be important, or that are repugnant to us, or that fall somewhere between; and that such values are both social and historical. This is not to say that such discussions are in no sense whatever aesthetic: rather, it is to insist that the aesthetic is not an autonomous category, but that we have to invoke it only when we begin to consider in what way music differs from life. Our need then, is to see that the apparently autonomous and absolute questions about music are not – and never have been – autonomous at all; we need to strip them of the self-sufficiency that they have in recent history acquired, and reduce them again to their *real* content. Once we are able to do that, we shall be on the way to taking music truly seriously. And that, I believe, can only help us to take the totality of life seriously. For me the two realms are inseparable. By elevating this relationship to full con-sciousness we may not only become better musicians; we may also, to paraphrase Handel, become better people.

NOTES

1) 'Criticism and Dogmatism in Literature', *Dialectics of Liberation* (ed. David Cooper), Penguin 1968, p. 131.

2) For example, his *Ways of Seeing*, Penguin 1972.

3) 'Schools of English and Contemporary Society', *The Use of English*, Vol. XV, Nos. 2 & 3, Winter '63/Spring '64, pp. 79-80.

4) 'Marx's Contribution to Historiography', *Ideology in Social Science*, (ed. Robin Blackburn), Fontana, London 1972, p.266.

5) 'History: the Poverty of Empiricism', *Ideology in Social Science, op. cit.*, p.113.

6) 'Music Historiography in Eastern Europe', *Perspectives in Musicology* (ed. Barry S. Brook, Edward O.D. Downes, and Sherman van Solkema), Norton, New York, 1972, pp.228, 236, 245-6.

7) 'American Musicology and the European Tradition', *Musicology* (by F.L. Harrison, M. Hood and C. Palisca), Englewood Cliffs, New Jersey, 1963, pp.79-80, and 6-8.

8) Quoted in Supičič, 'Instead of a Introductory Word', *International Review of Music Aesthetics and Sociology*, Vol. 1, No. 1, June 1970, p.4.

9) 'The Aesthetic Problems of the Renaissance', *Revue belge de musicologie*, Vol. IX, Nos. 3-4, 1955, p.84.

10) 'Music, the Unknown', *Musicology, op. cit.,* p.282.

11) 'What Should Musicology Be?', *Current Musicology*, Spring 1965, p.58.

12) 'American Musicology and the Social Sciences', *Perspectives in Musicology, op. cit.,* p.212.

13) 'Factorial Analysis of the Song as an Approach to the Formation of a Unitary Field Theory for Musicology', *Journal of the International Folk Music Council,* Vol XX, 1966, pp.33-39.

14) 'Musicology and Related Disciplines', *Perspectives in Musicology, op. cit.,* p.186.

15) 'Editorial', *Musical Quarterly,* Vol. L, No. 2., April 1964, pp. 215 and 223.

16) 'American Musicology and the European Tradition', *op. cit.*

17) See esp. 'Beethoven, Hegel and Marx', *Music Review,* Vol. 33, No. 1, February 1972, pp.34 to 46, reproduced in this book as Chapter II.

18) 'The Affirmative Character of Culture', *Negations,* Allen Lane, The Penguin Press, 1968, pp.98 and 114.

19) 'Analysis Today', *Musical Quarterly,* Vol. XLVI, No. 2, April 1960, p. 187.

20) *The Human Sciences and Philosophy,* Cape Editions, London, 1969, p.84.

21) 'Remarks on the Method of Art History', *Burlington Magazine,* Vol. XCI, February and March 1949, pp.49-52 and 73-75.

22) 'Art and Objective Truth', *Writer and Critic,* Merlin Press, London, 1970, pp.34-35.

23) *Ibid.,* p.36.

24) *Ibid.,* p.54.

Chapter II

Beethoven, Hegel
and Marx

MUSICOLOGY, to paraphrase Merleau-Ponty, manipulates its world and gives up living in it. Paradigmatically, it tends to reduce critical thought to a set of data-collecting techniques, treating each of its objects with infinite blandness as though it were an object-in-general – 'as though it meant nothing to us and yet was predestined for our own use'. Nothing in musicology's formal operational thinking asks it to understand its own foundations or to call them into question (at the one extreme); or (at the other) to disclose the human horizon of its endeavours – the value and meaning that presumably drench the objects that inhabit the world of its operations.

These limitations are most evident on those occasions when we should most be able to go beyond them. Such occasions include those when we find ourselves implicitly, and collectively on a large scale, reaffirming that a particular composer has relevance to us – as notably happens whenever we celebrate the anniversary of a composer's birth. But for us, the experts, these still remain on the whole purely formal, ascetic affairs. Having proclaimed the date, sent out the invitations and ordered the cake, we fail to turn up to suggest why we should be having a party at all. This was the lacuna at the heart of 1970's birthday festivities. We were commemorating Beethoven – but *why?* It is at once the most obvious and the most problematic of

30

questions; and perhaps we ignored it because we knew it would easily beg its answer: 'We are celebrating Beethoven because he is Beethoven'. Amid the array of impressive scholarly publications one looked in vain for attempts to come to grips frankly with the question of what kind of meaning a composer born on the brink of the French Revolution might possibly have for men and women living two-hundred years later in the age of space technology. Had we been pressed to answer, what might we have said? If we were called to account now, what would we say? Many of us, I think, would hope to suggest that the value of Beethoven's music for us has something to do with its involvement with life's most profound and searching dilemmas, with its striving to win through, to forge hope from hopelessness. Of course, these are rough-and-ready formulations. Nonetheless, I think they refer us correctly to the very heart of Beethoven's importance for us: namely – and this is what I shall discuss here – his articulation in music of the principle of dialectic in all its rich and splendid logical and affective significance.

Beethoven was eighteen at the start of the French Revolution, that momentous event which was all at once the testing ground and the stimulus for one of the great upheavals in human thought. Briefly, the significance of the Revolution was this. Through it people both demonstrated and comprehended for the first time that history and human nature were their own; that it was in their power to take back these things into their own hands, and to shape them for themselves. But central to this experience was the belief that the old social order had needed to be overthrown because it had come to express only a lie, and that it was the new order that had forged an access to the truth. The attempt to construe this in an adequate conceptual form led to the view that from time to time the obvious picture of 'reality', given by common sense as indisputable, is not true at all; rather, it is the very denial, or negation, of the truth. That is why it can be contradicted by other pictures of 'reality'. But where, then, *is* the truth? The answer is that the truth exists beyond, or behind, the present defamation of itself. And if the truth is to be grasped, all these stable but contradictory appearances – all these pictures – must themselves be negated, just as the *ancien regime* had been negated. The truth will then emerge as a new interpretation of reality, whose distinctive feature will be that it has taken up and re-embodied the original pictures in a more appropriate form: it will, in fact, be a synthesis of the earlier untruths. Now, at a certain stage this truth will also cease to be truly true; it will be contradicted and undergo the same process. Reality is thus seen as essentially contradictory, but the negation inherent in it is the principle of all life and movement.

It was Hegel, of course, who first elaborated these ideas into a total system, and one that is a living demonstration of the processes it describes. His metaphysic takes the stable categories of traditional formal logic and dissolves them into a restless sea of antagonisms: in this way it is itself an abolition of that logic and a synthesis dependent on it. Reality, in the view I have been describing, is dynamic: so Hegel's ontology is a flux, a ceaseless becoming, propelled by the clash of contradictory forces. But all this unrest *(Unruhe)* has a goal and finishing point. Its aim is rest, at the point where man, fully aware of these processes and his own part in them, is truly free. And this – 'the only pole of repose amid the ceaseless chain of events and conditions' – Hegel saw as the aim of the struggles of history.

It would be surprising if a relationship with reality as powerful and deeply rooted as the dialectic were not to find sensuous, artistic embodiment: and indeed the sonata principle is precisely the dialectic in its musical analogue. Sonata, which grew up around the time of the Revolution and sprang from the same impulse, is a way of musical thinking which generates contradictions between (say) opposing tonalities, themes, rhythmic characters, within the course of a single movement as well as over a multi-movement structure. Its starting point is the difference between the reality and the potentiality, exactly as in Hegel's dialectic. Sonata dramatizes the principle whereby something may become something else under the driving force of contradiction: it is the highest musical articulation of the idea of forward movement through conflict. One thinks immediately of the sonatas, symphonies and so on, of

Haydn, Mozart and Beethoven, as the highest embodiment of this principle; and so they are. But it is Beethoven – born in the same year as Hegel – who emerges as the most thoroughly 'Hegelian' of the three; it is he who pursues most relentlessly the dialectic of becoming, driving his thematic complexes through from what they are not but seem to be, to what they are but appear not to be. Haydn and Mozart do not attempt such radical reversals. Mozart can *begin* with spiritual blessedness; Beethoven must begin with cliches, rude, commonsensical – the currency of the obvious that, as for Hegel, offers only a deceptive 'security' – and find rest, which now takes on the character of triumph, only after a heroic struggle. We should not let the fact that both Mozart and Beethoven are dialecticians obscure their difference. What stands between them is the critical, formative experience of the Revolution: the final collapse of the late feudal order, and the demonstration that, against overwhelming odds, men can – and must – shape their own destinies.

The point I am trying to make will become clearer if I attempt some general distinctions between the music of the revolutionary sonata principle and the music it replaced. 'Formerly', said Balzac, 'the caste gave every person his physiognomy which dominated his individuality; today the individual receives his physiognomy from himself.' A remark of Beethoven's, addressed to his patron Prince Lichnowsky, is also apposite:

Prince, what you are you are by accident of birth; what I am, I am through my own efforts. There have been thousands of princes and there will be thousands more; there is only one Beethoven!

The musical style appropriate to the pre-Revolutionary conception of an unalterable human 'nature' was the Bachian principle of extension by varied, motor-like repetition; but the post-Revolutionary view of man as a product his own efforts called for nothing less than the full Beethovenian dialectic, the principle not of extension but of movement, of contradiction rather than repetition, and of thematic transformation rather than variation. Where, in the earlier style, a piece evolves on the basis of what is already there at the beginning, in the later it gropes ever towards a new formulation, one not given but latent within an original contradiction: it strives to become what it is *not*, on the basis of what it *is*.

Reason, in the Hegelian mind, is elevated to a position of supremacy, and therefore cannot tolerate a reality that is unreasonable to the degree to which it is defaced by contradictions. Refusing to be lulled – or more strictly, mystified – by the superficially placid and quiescent surfaces of things, reason hunts out the contradictions, knowing them to be the ignition points which can be exploded so as to shatter the stable, harmonious structure that common sense had assumed in order to canonize it. These are exactly the priorities and the procedures of sonata music, and they essentially distinguish it from the fugal style. Fugue reveres stability and unity. The working-out of a fugal subject demonstrates through the unity of counterpoint the capacity of the subject to integrate diverse experiences into the fundamental oneness of its spirit. Neither through modulation – which is to closely related keys, and is so handled that far from undermining the home key it confirms it as still primary – nor through thematic 'development' – which exhibits the potentialities of the subject matter – are the fugue's basic premises ever called into question. It runs a course in which it can afford to take risks because its monistic unshakability is guaranteed.

Sonata, on the other hand, aims from the start at duality. In the exposition one thematic-tonal area is contradicted by another. It is inadequate to speak of them (as is the custom) as 'contrasts', for that term evades precisely what is specific to sonata-type contrasts. They are not merely different subjects arbitrarily hitched together. Behind their evident surface (foreground) dissimilarity there is a latent (or background) identity which we feel though do not yet comprehend, and which gives them a relationship that is necessary rather than contingent. Analysis can easily disclose this identity (and in the work of such critics as Rudolph Reti frequently has) and so support the view that the sonata subjects are partial and contradictory (Hegelian) 'appearances' abstracted from the latent ground of a common totality. The subject-areas are contradictory 'pictures' of reality organized in and around individual subjective centres. Hegelian 'reason' goes to work on the contradiction in the so-called development. Here nothing is sacred. As the mind stretches itself to penetrate the surfaces of the competing pictures, it shatters the relative stability of the exposition's antagonistic views and may summon up as much of the syntactical and grammatical procedures of musical language as it finds necessary. It may dissect, analyze, examine, counterpose, combine, distort, and will probably release the explosive energy implied by the contradictions of the exposition. Here the competing certainties of the earlier part of the movement are ransacked, emptied of their 'security', their apparent 'truth' profoundly called into question. The development is as logical, rigorous and relentless, and as deeply immersed in the strains and stresses of contradiction, as the proper reasoning of a dialectical mind must be. What this experience discovers is passed on to the so-called recapitulation. This is no mere reprise or review, but a reworking of the earlier positions on a *new level,* such as is adequate to what the rationality of the development has disclosed. It must oppose everything that has gone before and yet must redeem it; it must give to the music the meaning to which the exposition pretended, but denied. Customarily, it retains enough of the exposition to show that it has reunited that section's opposing 'appearances' to the ground from which they were partial abstractions. This it will usually do principally by uniting the subject-groups in the terrain of the principal tonality, now newly enhanced – placed on another level – by the struggles that wrenched it from all that had previously denied it. Sometimes the development will have unmasked the surface opposition of the themes in favour of their underlying unity; in such cases our knowledge of that truth collaborates with the recapitulation's transcendence of duality. In Beethoven, the recapitulation's surpassing of the earlier conflicts is sometimes confirmed in thematic formulations that resolve figures that were formerly 'spoiled' by discordant inflections into simple, concordant, often triadic, structures: in Reti's instances, 'a line centred around a chord of the seventh is resolved into a triad, or a complex chordal progression into one rooted in the tonic-dominant relation'. It is not far-fetched to see in this sonata process of exposition, development, and recapitulation, a rough correspondence to the path of the Hegelian search for truth, which sets out from sense-knowledge or sense-certainty, and passes through perception before arriving at understanding and finally self-knowledge. Sonata, moreover, like the unifying of opposites in Hegel, ends only when reason has organized the whole so that 'every part exists only in relation to the whole', and 'every individual entity has meaning and significance only in its relation to the totality'. The replacement of stable fugue subjects by unstable sonata subjects belongs intimately to the movement that dissolved the stable categories of traditional formal logic into the unstable dynamic of a philosophy whose forms shift and swirl about under the stresses of contradiction.

The conflict between subjects in sonata is homologous with the Hegelian necessary determination of self through struggle with others, a struggle which ultimately passes over – as it does in recapitulation – into a harmonious mutual affirmation. Hegel saw this conflict archetypically in the struggle – famous in his description of it – between the master and the servant. In sonata this notion arrives in music for the first time as necessary and fundamental. The continuous multi-layered counterpoint of (say) fugue *assumes* a harmonious, ordered totality in which each line 'supports' the others, and in which all are necessary to each only in that they help to provide the context where each will take its place and from which it will derive the meaning already etched out for it *in advance*. The revolutionary sonata view wants nothing to do with this assumption. It negates it with the experience of contradiction and (especially by the time of Beethoven) of conflict that is basic to it and is its whole provenance, opposing subject to subject, movement to movement, for the purpose – through mutual antagonism – of mutual definition and growth. 'By myself', says Merleau-Ponty in an essay on Hegel, 'I cannot be free, nor can I be a consciousness or a man'; but sonata (again especially with Beethoven) retains as its *hope* the general condition that fugue was able to assume, but knows that its coming to life shall be possible only when the 'affirmation of self which is the principle behind the struggle' yields the realization that 'my consciousness of another as an enemy comprises an affirmation of him as an equal'; when struggle transforms itself into coexistence through the comprehension that 'the other whom I first saw as my rival is a rival only because he is myself'. The tonal and thematic resolution of a Beethoven sonata movement is homologous with the experience in which 'I discover myself in the other'.

This notion of the necessary conflict between determinate beings involves in a special way the concept of *limit*. For Hegel, to exist is to have limits *(Grenzen)* beyond which a being ceases to be what it is, and against which it perpetually presses in order to become what it is not. Hegel speaks of this as 'the unrest of something in its limits'. In a process of perpetual becoming, being is ever knocking down and surpassing these barriers only to confront new ones. The limited nature of being through its relation to other beings is thus the very root of contradiction and the source of the dynamic of life. With this concept of limit we arrive at one of Hegel's most revolutionary ideas. Through it, he liberated thought from the religious influences to which it had been subject even in its secular eighteenth-century forms. Before Hegel, 'limit' implied 'sinfulness'; things were finite and consorted with negativity because they had fallen from a state of grace. For Hegel, however, the limitation of things is no longer an unfortunate aspersion on them: it is a characteristic so fundamentally basic to them that without it they could not even exist; it is the generator of their movement, the fount of their strength, the very realm of their truth. This change expresses one of the profound differences between Baroque fugue and Classical sonata. The former disdains the fixed and finite structure of the melodic period; it aspires to a *melos* that defies limits, striving to be continuous and, in principle, without end. Sonata is founded upon limit. Where fugue is an 'open' form, sonata is 'closed', and holds within itself many smaller 'closed' forms: the Classical period is the great age of the cadence. Sonata is structured; its thematic material is based paradigmatically on the symmetrical period with a beginning, middle and end, and the music grows through the contradiction and complementation of antecedent and consequent phrases, sentences, paragraphs, sections, and finally whole movements. Boundaries are its essence. Its life is a perpetual birth and a perpetual perishing – what to C. P. E. Bach around the time of the first appearance of sonata seemed a kind of 'juggling': 'Hardly', he said, 'has the executant musician stilled one emotion than he excites another; thus does he juggle with the passions'.

Underlying this discussion is the assumption that Beethoven is more 'Hegelian' than Haydn or Mozart. Later, we shall find ourselves qualifying this view; but for the moment we can consider further Beethoven's close relationship to Hegel by thinking about his attitude to chaos. The tendency of Beethoven's subjects to take chaos upon themselves for the sake ultimately of defeating chaos – especially during development – is another point of intersection of his art with the philosophy of Hegel; it represents symbolically, as in the aspect of musical history, what Beethoven's creative enterprise did actually – the calling of the 'world-historical individual'. Hegelian heroes are unlike all previous heroes. They act without the guarantee of the compensations of Providence and in opposition to the established moral and social order of their time. They defy the system because, alone, they see that it has outlived itself. Of the future they want they can have no knowledge except that in the passion of their response to what they acutely perceive in the present, they constitute that future in their hearts as a just and a passionate demand, and as the only possible way of wrenching a meaning from the present. It is a vision to which they will sacrifice all personal happiness and security. Hegel speaks of 'an underground source in the inner spirit whose content is hidden and which has not yet broken through the surface of actual existence, but which strikes against the outer world as against a shell and cracks it because such a shell is unsuited to such kernel. . .' This 'underground source' is the spring from which Hegel's heroes draw their 'goals and their vocation'; but Beethoven's themes drink from this spring too, propelling themselves onward toward another present which lies ahead of them but which they must make by a huge effort to transformation. Through an act of will and imagination the thematic material of the finale of the Ninth Symphony brings itself into being by deriving itself (as Reti has shown) from the symphony's foregoing themes; the exultant D major finally realizes a vision that was in part glimpsed – or rather, imagined – more than once in the D minor and B flat contexts of the rest of the symphony. The finale incarnates a future (now a present) grasped in the midst of the present (now a past) as its objective possibility. The inner spirit has finally broken through the surface. The kernel has exploded the shell. Only to make this process quite explicit the baritone protagonist near the beginning of the finale summons forth the new order in the midst of a portrayal of chaos. He is Hegel's 'world-historical individual', and Beethoven; the spirit of sonata speaking for the first and only time, and the first of Hegel's 'new race' about whom 'one might say they. . . already existed within the old. . .'

Beethoven is Hegel's 'world-historical individual' in the sense that he stands at the beginning of the modern era which – however much its subsequent development may have betrayed his hopes – he helped to inaugurate. He is the first modern composer because he is the first to confront a universe whose order he could neither believe in nor – even if it existed – accept. He is the first composer to inhabit a world without certainties. Chaos is real or immanent and in the task of facing it neither Church nor State will be able to offer any succour because the chasm has opened up under their feet. Order is no longer vouchsafed; and there is a precise correlation between this fact and the corrosion of musical conventions that we recognize in the increase in the number and type of verbal or shorthand 'instructions' Beethoven feels it necessary to provide for his interpreters. Bach needed to give few or no instructions; even the highly subjective gestures of Haydn and Mozart wanted only a minimum of directions before they could be properly understood, since they were expressions upon a countenance whose general features and character were well known through having been sketched out by intensive common practice. Beethoven's face wears a different expression. As his eyes look into the chasm to see what men have not seen before, his brow furrows in a new way, the line of his jaw sets with a determination still so novel as to be frightening. Without the welter of instructions strung together, the Italian and German terms, the metronome markings, the finely indicated dynamics, we could not know what it is precisely that he sees, or what those lines portend, or – could it be possible? – why the corners of the eyes soften humourously, and the lie of the features betokens a peace in spite of it all.

I began by writing about truth, about how in the revolutionary, dialectical view truth is on the losing side and has to be won by a special kind of effort. I hope it is becoming clear that music discloses exactly the same shift in attitude.

A subject of Beethoven's is a proposition whose truth emerges only out of its sonata activity: it is posited in order to be contradicted by another subject, and after its negation preserved in synthesis with its opposition on a higher level. Its essence, or what Hegel would have called its 'notion', resides only in its totality; it *becomes* its essence, its essence is not given to it. Where Bach is static, then, Beethoven is dynamic. But their relationship is a dialectical one, and to be accurate we must express it in a more complex way. We must say that in Beethoven's dynamic of becoming the stasis of Bach is simultaneously refuted and preserved – or *aufgehoben*, to use Hegel's word. In just the same way, Hegel's dialectic is a surpassing of the old formal and stable analytic.

I want to take two very well-known pieces by Beethoven and try to give some hint of the marvellous way dialectic operates in them. Broadly speaking, the Fifth Symphony moves from the doom-laden first movement to the exultation of the last by making that fateful four-note motif itself yield the theme of triumph: without the despair there is no rejoicing. The symphony seems to support what Beethoven once said in a letter: 'We finite ones with infinite souls are born only for sorrows and joy, and it might almost be said that the best of us receive joy through sorrow'. The critical point in the symphony's dialectical process is the passage in which the scherzo yields the finale. After the trio, the scherzo has returned, chilled to around freezing point. It is utterly expressionless; its frightening, unstoppable kinetic energy confronting us nakedly with a power that seems the very negation of the human world. Soon the music is close to extinction, melodyless, motionless except for that four-note rhythm – which has been predominant throughout – on the kettledrum. But – and this is the vital Hegelian moment – it is this very extremity that liberates the impulse that is to transform the C minor scherzo into the glorious C major finale in fifty bars. At this lowest point it is the main scherzo theme *itself* that is the subject of a tremendous striving, twisting itself into an upward spiral that cancels minor with major before exploding into the new theme. Furthermore, the four-note rhythm on the kettledrum becomes a steady pounding that never leaves the note C. C was the tonal root of this area of negation, and now, where most other composers would have dropped the kettledrum onto the dominant, Beethoven keeps it prominently on the tonic; he wants us to apprehend how even the very root and ground of negation is an essential constituent of the ground of affirmation; how the C of the minor-mode scherzo is annihilated and preserved – or *aufgehoben* – by the C of the triumphant major-mode finale. It is impossible to escape the conclusion that here victory has been wrought out of the very stuff of defeat. 'I will grapple with Fate', wrote Beethoven; 'it shall not quite bear me down: oh, it is lovely to live life a thousand times!' The connection in this sentence between the 'grappling with Fate' and the 'lovliness of life' gives it a movement which makes no sense at all except in terms of the same processes we have seen at work in the Fifth Symphony. So that we can truly grasp that these opposites now exist in a state of identity, the scherzo makes a brief reappearance in the heart of the finale: and this union is Hegel's condition of truth. For here the negative has not, to use his words, 'been thrown away, like dross from pure metal – nor even as the tool is excluded from the finished vessel;

rather. . . the negative . . . [is] still immediately present in the true as such'. Another passage in Hegel seems to give expression to a principle profoundly at one with the transitional bars I have been talking about:

> . . . the spirit. . . matures slowly and quietly toward the new form, dissolving one particle of the edifice of its previous world after the other, while its tottering is suggested only by some symptoms here and there: . . . the indeterminate apprehension of something unknown. . . harbingers of a forthcoming change. This gradual crumbling which did not alter the physiognomy of the whole is interrupted by the break of day that, like lightning, all at once reveals the edifice of the new world.

Perhaps an even clearer example of the long-range operation of musical dialectic is provided by the Seventh Symphony. In this piece, a complex contradiction is clarified by being broken down into its components in the first three movements before being resolved in the fourth. Recall the slow introduction: it is here that the original contradiction is presented; but vaguely, problematically. The introduction is a welter of contradictory urges. Thematic motives generate strange, baffling consequences, none of which achieves any fulfilment; and the contradictions are tonal as much as they are thematic, for the main key of a A major is quickly undermined by its own totally unexpected implications of C major and F major – areas of antagonism in relation to the main key. What *is* this confusion of thematic and tonal tendencies? What is the relationship between the conflicting segments? Why do they frustrate each other? How can the opposing interests be led to fulfilment and at the same time reconciled? How can a condition of harmony be attained, given such logical antagonisms? This is the problem the symphony faces. If the complex contradiction is to be abolished, adequate awareness of its constituents must first be gained, and it is this that the symphony sets out to do by taking up the introduction in analogous tonal and thematic terms. Patiently, rationally, the introduction is 'composed out' over four movements, and in the process it is fulfilled, comprehended and transcended.

The first movement suppresses thematic conflict in order to

concentrate on tonal conflict: the movement is a vast struggle between the home key of A, and non-A, which attempts to undermine the huge areas belonging to A and so disrupt their dance and song. The slow movement, in turn, releases thematic opposition and suppresses tonal opposition: the alternating sections contrast thematically but have a key-centre (A) in common, and in common with the previous movement also. Now a synthesis is made: the first two movements are *aufgehoben* by the scherzo, which poses the the contradiction – for the first time in the symphony – in unambigious tonal *and* thematic terms. It only poses it, statically: yet the fact that it has been clarified means that it is only a step away from its ultimate negation; and the finale, at the very moment it dynamically takes up the contradiction in all its clarity, also transcends it by making the inherent tension the source of its own dionysian vitality.

My argument has placed Beethoven beside Hegel, but it cannot leave him there. Hegel was not the last word in dialectics. If his aim was human self-realization, his idealism provided no means of tackling this problem in any other than an abstract, speculative way. Here is philosophy enchanted by itself: the driving force of history turns out to be pure thought, or a phantom that Hegel conjures up as 'World-Spirit' – but certainly not real people, who are merely the agents of this *Weltgeist*. This must not sound like a dismissal of Hegel. If his dialectic was an abstract, logical attempt to catch hold of the movement of life – which failed because it was abstract – then all it needed to make it truly adequate to its specific historical task was for it to be filled with real, concrete content. It needed, in its own terms, to be negated and recreated. Putting this differently, we might say that in Hegel the dialectic is standing on its head. Karl Marx saw this; and the image is his. 'To rise', he said, 'it is not enough to do so *in thought* and to leave hanging over our *real sensual* head the *real palpable* yoke that cannot be subtilzed away with ideas.'

Now I want to suggest that Beethoven was standing on his feet from the beginning; that he was, so to speak, Marx to his own Hegel. Marx accused Hegel of lacking 'flesh and sinew'.

But Beethoven already *had* this 'flesh and sinew', because the idiom he forged for himself was nothing if not warm-blooded, reverberating with sensual, palpitating life. And even more than his predecessors, Beethoven declared the roots of his art to lie in real, affective existence, and chose its raw materials from the stamping of dancing feet, the cries and songs of common people. Once he explicitly said that music was a mingling of the spiritual and the sensuous.

But this notion – of the fusion of the spiritual and the sensuous, or of the theoretical and the practical – was crucial to Marx' placing of the dialectic firmly on its feet. Marx held that true consciousness of the world is consciousness of the way we shape the world and are shaped by it. Therefore it is self-consciousness: an awareness of ourselves in the world, making it on the basis of certain given conditions and being made by it, but always implicated in it, body and mind, ineluctably, whether we like it or not. And once we have understood this we have forever united theory to practice. For theory is the understanding that grasps the world: the grasping is already the practice that changes it. Here we have what Marx called *praxis*.

It is a comprehension that is already implicit in the music of Beethoven. In Beethoven, for the first time, music no longer presents itself as a mere reflection of the world, but as simultaneously an engaged response to it and as a summons to change it. I am not thinking here only of the military idiom, encountered so frequently, and particularly in the concertos, nor only of the Ninth Symphony's final resort to the full density of verbal exhortation. What I really have in mind is the sense that we have, in listening to Beethoven, that the struggles of his music begin and end with the concrete struggles of real life. Think of the way the difficulties of his music are spiritual *and* physical. There is a special relationship between these two seemingly opposite aspects which is, in the profoundest Marxian sense, dialectical. Neither of the two is prior to the other or can exist meaningfully without it: in fact, spiritual and physical gains mediate each other. Take some of the obvious practical conquests demanded by his music: a victory over a keyboard, over the limitations of the human body, over the physical limitations of a musical instrument. These are all physical achievements which yield an enriched spirituality, but which themselves pre-suppose this very same spiritual achievement and are impossible without it. As nowhere else in music, these two seemingly opposite spheres coincide and generate each other: it is a kind of enhanced symbiosis. And when it is fully understood it means that the music is at the same time more than itself, because it strains all the time toward the world from which it erupted, going, as it came, as *praxis*. Never before had music been so mentally *and* physically rousing; in Beethoven thought and affect are inextricably welded to action.

The 'materiality' of the Marxian and the Beethovenian *praxis* gives their projected culmination of the dialectic a quite different character from that which the final *Aufhebung* has in Hegel – or, for that matter, in Haydn and Mozart. Hegel and Mozart tend to be quietistic and conservative where Marx and Beethoven are activistic and revolutionary. For Hegel, thought can accomplish the project of history – and indeed has already done so. For Marx, thought can avail nothing unless it is linked to a rebuilding of the material framework – the economic relations – of society from the foundations up. Hegel's eschatology is an idealistic apotheosis, accomplished silently; Marx's is the millenium of the real world, a tumultuous rejoicing following upon 'a total redemption of humanity'. We can grasp this by understanding the specific nature of the treatment which both Marx and Beethoven give to the concept of 'return'. In sonata, 'return' means recapitulation, or the summary and synthesis of finale: the simultaneous taking up and surpassing of the original contradictions which were symbolic of the estrangement of man from man, and of the alienation of man from his own true self and from nature. This 'return' is nothing other than 'a complete and conscious return which assimilates all the wealth of previous development', in the words with which Marx speaks of the putative new order, and which equally well describe the principle of sonata 'return'. But only the context of those words fully gives away the tone of triumph and exultation that belongs to the Marxian apocalypse. The new order, says Marx, is the abolition not only of private property, but also

of human self-alienation, and [is] thus the real appropriation of human nature through and for man. It is, therefore, the return of man to himself as a social, *i.e.* really human, being, a complete and conscious return which assimilates all the wealth of previous development. [This order] as fully developed naturalism is humanism, and as fully developed humanism is naturalism. It is the definitive resolution of the antagonism between man and nature, and between man and man. It is the true solution of the conflict between existence and essence, between objectification and self-affirmation, between freedom and necessity, between individual and species. It is the solution of the riddle of history and knows itself to be this solution.

To those who have responded fully to the music, this 'return' is the triumphant millennium of the finale of the Fifth and Ninth symphonies (to keep only to works already cited); and it is a 'return' unknown to the sonata principle before Beethoven.

But in his treatment of this 'return' Beethoven goes beyond Marx who, though he replaced Hegel's idea of 'reason' with the idea of 'happiness', never spoke about the future society he hoped for, except in a vague and general way. But with music it is a different matter altogether. Music is a purely connotative symbolism, not denotative like ordinary language; that is why it can do as much as Beethoven does and still not become a fiction. It can negate the present in such a way that, as Sartre put it, it speaks to men of their sorrows in the same voice which they will use to speak of them when they are comforted. It can remember the present from the standpoint of the promised future, and so bring to us the *feeling* of that future.

Take the 'Arietta' of the last piano sonata. Or better still, let us think of any of the fugal syntheses that occur so frequently in Beethoven's late music. These fugal movements belong to his final statements on the sonata principle and on the idea of alienation it dramatizes: and now Beethoven at once posits and abolishes both concepts. Themes cease to be disjunct and contradictory. Instead, they realize a new totality by becoming mutually supportive. By the same stroke there is no longer a thematic foreground over a harmonic background, but these divisions are *aufgehoben* by the indivisible totality of thematic lines whose simultaneity and mutual necessity *are* the harmony. Truly, it is a case of the free development of each becoming a condition of the free development of all—Marx's words.

Beethoven's fugues differ from Bach's in that they are dialectical syntheses. Bach could write counterpoint because his faith rendered the present alienation irrelevant; but Beethoven *started* from alienation, then in musical terms transcended it.

This makes it clear that Beethoven's aspirations echo those of Hegel and Marx; that is to say, man's re-appropriation of himself and the fulfilment of history. But Beethoven has been dead a hundred and fifty years, and in the meantime he has had many successors, and, in the fullest sense, virtually no inheritors. Contradiction and the dialectical pursuance of it were alive in the age of the French Revolution because they were part of the consciousness and the lived experience of a social class who were interested in deep social, and personal, change and in the unbroken and purposeful generation of a genuinely democratic order. This state of affairs did not last. The defeat of the Revolution of 1848 only confirmed and set the seal on a trend that had been gathering pace for some time: the betrayal by the *bourgeoisie* of the democratic ideals which they themselves originally formulated and the erasure of dialectic from all forms of thought. History, for instance, lost its contradictory character and came to be seen as smooth and uneventful evolution; economics forgot what in its 'classical' phase it had known about the contradictions of the capitalist system, and now pretended to a harmonious functionality; philosophy turned its back on Hegel because the dialectic contained 'the principle of revolution'. Music was not exempt. But for rare exceptions, music abandoned a sonata style so rigorous – and when it is less than rigorous it is something else – that it owed each of its motions to the logical unfolding and working-out of contradiction, and concluded this process in a final *Aufhebung* that depended on everything that had gone before.

The abandonment of dialectic prompts a reflection on the

paradoxical position of Beethoven today. He is the first modernist, but he is virtually without heirs. He is the most popular of the great composers but perhaps the one who is the least understood in the *specific* nature of his message. Certainly, he is popular at a time when this content would be rejected even if it were understood – a contingency in any case well guarded against by the musicological positivism of the academic watchdogs to whose 'expertise' the task has been entrusted of reifying music into an *object* and proscribing as 'nonsense' any musical enquiry other than the 'scientific' collection of data.

In what, then, does Beethoven's popularity reside? Perhaps it is in the hope of happiness he offers to an unhappy world, however much the abstractness of an interpretation such as this etherializes the specificity of the music's content. But for those who really care, this also defines our task: to insist, in opposition to all resistances, on the true and concrete nature of this content, which is within reach of our understanding because we belong still to Beethoven's age, to the period inaugurated by the French Revolution whose finest ideals have been handed down to each succeeding generation as a still unanswered challenge. The measure of our fidelity to Beethoven's music will surely be the degree to which we find ourselves unable at this moment in history to listen to the music except with an agitated conscience.

Chapter III

Social and Philosophical Outlook in Mozart's Operas

Of all the tasks awaiting us in the social interpretation of msuic, that of Mozart would be the most difficult and the most urgent. T. W. Adorno, *Introduction to the Sociology of Music.*

Do MOZART's works reveal any of the features of a world-view? The question would seem to be both interesting and fundamental enough to be at least worth asking. Yet among the millions of words spawned by Mozartean scholarship, there is little to suggest that the question has been seriously posed, still less attempted in any systematic manner. Certainly Mozart is not the only composer whose *oeuvre* has not been interrogated in this way: musicology, which in the main construes itself and its world positivistically, is not predisposed to look into questions of this kind. And it is equally certain that such questions, once asked, will not easily yield their answers. A full discussion of the meta-musicological issues surrounding this problematic however, falls outside the purpose of this essay.

My intention, instead, is to attempt to show that at least some of Mozart's works *do* have features which bespeak a certain way of seeing and being in the world. For the sake of methodological simplicity, the discussion will be confined to his five greatest comic operas: *Die Entführung aus dem Serail, Le Nozze di Figaro, Don Giovanni, Cosi fan tutte,* and *Die Zauberflöte.* My contention will be that at least three major and interrelated philosophical themes run through these works; and that these are sufficiently in evidence to be regarded as important features of a general world-view that these five works take up and articulate, each in its own very different way. What follows is therefore not an exhaustive description of a Mozar-

49

tean philosophy. It is, rather, a first attempt to elucidate – and sociologically to account for – a few of its more striking characteristics as they appear in some of the composer's greatest dramatic works.

I

The five operas give numerous and diverse demonstrations of the thesis that the way social reality seems to be is not the way it 'really' is: that the conventional arrangements men and women find themselves in, and to which they seem bound – the structure of their conventional expectations, rules, institutions, and so on – frequently belie both the deeper dynamics which motivate them, and the fundamental truths about themselves and each other. These external forms, hardened by social approval and custom but concealing a more vital, more essential level of reality, constitute a kind of *mask*. In their activity in the world, men and women tend to see only these masks – their own and each other's, as well as the masks that screen the 'real' relationships between themselves. Mozart's major comic operas are scrupulously critical of these masks: they discover them in the manifold varieties and situations in which they occur, and then they strip them away. My – or rather, Mozart's – first theme, then, is the stripping away of masks. I shall deal with this theme by looking at a few salient examples in the five operas, taken in chronological order.

In *Die Entführung aus dem Serail,* the earliest of the five works, the theme of unmasking appears without the complexity of some of its later manifestations; its form is embryonic. In this opera reality is masked by one powerful and essential circumstance: in the opera's sixteenth-century Turkish palace it is decreed that Constanze shall love Selim, and that Blonde shall love Osmin. Indeed, a tyrannical *force* is one of the themes of the opera, epitomized most clearly in the character of Osmin. 'I command you to fall in love with me this very moment', he tells Blonde; and in the vaudeville finale to the last act, he imposes his will on the music, forcing it back to what he had sung in the first act. But one aspect of what the opera demonstrates is that feelings 'go' very differently from what force expects of them. What is unmasked is the true potential of human emotions: namely, that feelings are 'for themselves', they have their own life, they are not susceptible to arbitrary rule of any kind. In the process, what is also revealed is the human nobility of the two pairs of lovers – those who, in abject conditions, keep faith with the inclinations of their hearts against the dictates of authority. Significantly, in view of the theme of force—where attempts are made to 'force' love rather to 'seduce' it – the plan by which the lovers hope to escape is founded upon the seduction of one of the tyrants (Osmin) by wine. Apart from its comic value, this fact has ironic and highly suggestive import.

An unmasking is a revelation; and the idea of revelation is endemic to the sonata style as such, in which themes or motifs reveal the true potential that lies concealed behind their early appearance or surface manifestations. A fine, if simple, example of the operation of this principle occurs at the beginning of *Die Entführung*. The overture includes a brief, slower C minor section; its material is only stated, not explicated or developed. The overture evolves finally into the first number of the opera, Belmonte's C major aria of longing for Constanze, based on the motif from the C minor section of the overture. Here, however, that motif is further developed – revealed – and this, together with its major-key manifestation, seems at the same time to reveal an aspect of Belmonte's real feeling which was not evident in the undeveloped, minor-key appearance of the motif in the overture. Retrospectively the C minor episode in the overture 'stands for' Belmonte's given, sad predicament – his separation from his beloved. It is the appearance, his objective situation. The aria, however, reveals to us the less predictable, less static, more complex reality that lies within Belmonte's subjective grasp. It is his experience of hope.

In *Le Nozze di Figaro* the processes of masking and un-masking are rather more complex and ironic. To begin with, many of the masks are literal ones – pretences consciously adopted to mask a person or a situation: Cherubino dresses up and pretends not to be in Susanna's room; the Countess pretends that Susanna is in her dressing room; Figaro pretends to have jumped from the window; Figaro pretends to make love to the Countess, who is actually Susanna pretending to be the Countess; Susanna pretends to accept the Count's approaches; and so on. While at one level the very profusion of these masks reveals a world in which pretence and oblique communication are the norms, at another level they are untruths that sometimes contain a grain, or more than a grain, of truth. Thus, for example, Figaro's simulation of love for the Countess is 'true' as a potential: for, as the directness and the only superficially feigned sincerity of the music tells us, he could, given different circumstances, come to love her. The comedy of masks here more than hints at *Cosi fan tutte*. Figaro's normal relationship with the Countess is thus his *conventional* mask; this is stripped away from him by means of his pretence (the assumption of another mask) of love for the Countess, a 'lie' that threatens the 'truth' of his conventional mask, at the same time that it succeeds in unmasking the Count's indifference towards his wife and revealing his real feelings for her.

Another example is the scene in which Susanna and the Countess dress Cherubino as a girl. The delicacy and warmth of the music, its tittilating decorative figures, above all the rapturous pianissimo hush and static oscillation of violin and cello figures over dominant and tonic chords as Susanna admires the 'handsome little rascal' with his 'roguish glances' – all this speaks captivatingly of Susanna's erotic feelings for Cherubino. But in this very moment his sex changes: he is robed as a girl and complimented on his feminine good looks. In the process our notions of sexuality are teased and questioned to the point where they cease to have conventional meaning. Throughout the opera, Cherubino occupies a position somewhere between conventional sexual polarities – not least because he is a 'male' who sings with a 'female' voice.

What is most suggestively unmasked in Mozart's next opera, *Don Giovanni*, is the limitation of an ethical norm held by the society Mozart puts on his stage. Giovanni, evil and destructive though he is, is revealed to us as having a vigour and dynamism beyond that of any of the other characters. In a sense that we shall explore more fully later, he has – in spite of his conventionally destructive role – a power to quicken those around him, and to quicken them in direct proportion to the extent to which they genuinely enter into experience with him. In a complex way, then, the moralistic view of Giovanni is shown to be lacking, limited: it is unmasked as such by Mozart's opera. What is revealed is a more profound truth, the terms of which are that the hero and what he symbolizes have a strange and paradoxical creative force. George Bernard Shaw appositively commented about *Don Giovanni* that 'the only immoral feature of it is its supernatural retributive morality', and went on to add: 'Nor is it yet by any means an established fact that the world owes more to its Don Ottavios than to its Don Juans.'[1] The opera thus also gives the lie to the Manichean view that evil exists 'out there', totally split off from contact with the good. On the contrary, the opera exposes to us not only the inseparability of these principles but their constantly mingled and shifting interrelationship, and indeed the very relative nature of our categorization of them. Perhaps this is nowhere clearer than in the character of Leporello and his relationship with Giovanni. Despite the servant's oft-expressed dislike of his master, and Giovanni's complementary scorn for him, they really are a team, a unit. In Otto Rank's words :

We cannot imagine Don Juan without his servant and helper Leporello. This is not only a consequence of their actual dependence on each other as expressed in the plot, but is much more an intuitive sense of their psychological connection as a poetic effect... the figure of Leporello is a necessary part of the artistic presentation of the hero himself.[2]

At moments the connection becomes almost explicit: the catalogue aria, where the music bespeaks Leporello's braggardly identification with his master's accomplishments; Leporello's flirtings with the peasant girls as Giovanni pays his first attentions to Zerlina; Giovanni's admiration for the slick way Leporello plied Masetto and his friends with lies and drink and then took care of Elvira; the servant's Giovanni-esque adroitness is escaping from dangerous situations. In short, Leporello emerges as the 'poor man's Giovanni': as such he reveals to us the Giovanni in us all.

In Mozart's operas the condition of being masked – as well as the consequent unmasking – is often most powerfully suggested by the subtlest of musical means. In *Cosi fan tutte* there are many instances of this. Not for nothing are the first arias of Fiordiligi and Dorabella in *seria* style. Here, as frequently happens elsewhere, Mozart uses the archaic musical gestures of *opera seria* to symbolize situations in which people construe themselves or their world in antiquated ways – situations in which they act in a manner not in keeping with the more progressive and humane view of the late eighteenth century. In the earlier part of *Cosi,* the sisters are less in touch with the real, on-going life of their feelings than with somewhat outmoded notions such as honour, dignity, status and duty. In seeking to give voice to static 'affections' – affectations – rather than endeavouring to represent the more real and complex dynamic movement of their emotions, they were, for Mozart's time, committing an important deceit. Not only did they hark back to an older psychology, but also to an older and virtually superseded dispensation. Their first arias, in which they express these static and somewhat artificial emotions – heroic anguish unto death for Dorabella, rock-like fidelity for Fiordiligi – are set, significantly, in the *seria* manner. The women's engagement with the world at this moment is made in terms of an assumed and respectable convention; their music is rigid, dignified, severe, abrupt – traits which the women certainly might have (amongst others), but which do not wholly express what they most truly are, or might become. Their real possibilities, and hence the truth about their present condition, are masked. And the contradiction between protestations and possibilities is made more vivid by what we already *know:* Dorabella, in the earlier duet with her sister, had looked at the portrait of her lover and discerned there not only allure but also – confirmed by a sustained shudder in the music – menace; and then the sisters went on to speak of new stirrings, even mischief, in their hearts. Characteristically, of course, such presentiments were immediately repressed. The subsequent course of the opera may be seen as a slow laying bare of these very possibilities.

As the process of unmasking takes place, it is again the music that plays the most revelatory role. When the sisters for the first time decide to succumb to the flatteries of their new suitors, their decision is introduced by Dorabella as having the intention 'to amuse ourselves a little' and not to 'die of boredom'—which, she adds, 'is not to be false' since their hearts 'will stay as they are'. In the ensuing duet ('Prenderò quel brunettino') their words confirm this view: it will be mere sport, a joke. But the music tells us something different: exquisitely sensuous, graceful and lovely, what it really reveals is the rapturous frisson of a burgeoning erotic involvement. 'I'll imitate the other's sighs', Fiordiligi jests; but the music declares that the sighing is genuine. At its end the duet is a sublimely honeyed warbling.

The sense in which the course of the opera is an unmasking is articulated in plain terms by Alfonso. 'I deceived you', he tells the women when all has been revealed, 'but my deception undeceived your lovers, who henceforth will be wiser.' Deception undeceives; and undeception is wisdom. To be wise, you must deceive deception. Using a slightly different image, Joseph Kerman sees the original masks as shells: 'the opera seems to show a pair of rather unconscious couples tried and drawn a little way out of their conventional shells of sentimentality, proffered suicides, lockets, and parallel thirds.'[3]

In *Die Zauberflöte*, the play of masks touches directly upon social norms and the socially defined status of the various participants in the opera. At first we are presented with a mundane, conventional view of the truth; we think, as does Tamino, that the Queen of the Night is good and that Sarastro is evil. Our view of the truth is veiled – or indeed masked – just as are the faces of the Queen and her ladies, and just as the heads of the initiates will be (on Sarastro's orders) at the beginning of their trials. During the course of the opera, however, the passage away from an 'unredeemed' state is marked by the lifting of the veil for those who qualify: we, and the initiates, come to see another reality which supersedes the first. Only the Queen and her accomplices remain unenlightened, trapped in darkness behind their veils. This is not, as Jacques Chailley has suggested, a notion of the opera that owes more to Pirandello and the cinema of Alain Resnais than to the conventions of Mozart's time;[4] it is, to be precise, a dialectical view of reality that grew out of the lived experience of men and women in the late eighteenth century, that was rooted in their growing, crystallizing sense of the movement of history, and in their understanding of the dynamic and contingent nature of what people take to be their 'truths'.

In this opera, as in others, we have again a situation where the stripping away of masks rests to a very significant degree upon musical means. The Queen of the Night affords a clear example of this. In her first aria she sings of her motherly love for her poor abducted daughter; in her second aria this has been replaced by a singleminded and chilling dedication to revenge, in the throes of which she threatens to cast her daughter from her affections. And it is the music which makes plain that the emotions expressed in the second aria are the more real, the deeper. The consequences of our discoveries about the Queen during the opera are that she 'falls from grace' in our eyes, as well as in the eyes of the initiates. This trajectory is both aided and charted *inter alia* by the keys in which her moments of song are situated and their relationship to the 'redeemed' or 'enlightened' key of E flat major, with its Masonic three flats. Her first aria is in B flat and G minor – one flat less than E flat's three; her second in D minor – with the flats depleted now to one. Her final appearance at the end of the opera we should expect to be in C major, with no flats at all – which it nearly is, by being in C *minor:* and most appropriately so, for the dramatic situation requires a dark tonal area, and C minor is 'dark' with respect both to C major (of which it is the enharmonic minor) and to the triumphal E flat major (of which it is the relative minor).

Another 'revelation', resting to a comparable extent upon musical devices, concerns Pamina and Papageno. Situated in G minor – as was Pamina's tragic 'Ach, ich fühl's – Papageno's decision to commit suicide makes contact with Pamina's. They also share a metre ($\frac{6}{8}$) and a simple homophonic accompaniment. Mozart thereby demonstrates a common humanity beneath the otherwise significant differences between these two characters, confirming the potentiality for shared experience that had been suggested in their early duet, 'Bei Männern welche Liebe fühlen'. In these passages, among them some of the most 'felt' and moving moments in the opera, Mozart has again stripped away surfaces, socially conditioned and condoned appearances, to reveal the essential underlying but normally concealed reality.

II

The second notable theme in Mozart's operas, to be considered here, springs naturally from the first; it has, however, more obviously philosophical import. It is the dialectical view that the so-called 'negative' is necessary for its creative potential. In less abstract terms, this might be expressed by saying that without the darker sides of human experience, the brighter are not possible; that without destruction there can be no real creation; that without death there is no life; and that life, therefore, to be truly alive, must be a kind of permanent revolution. This idea, or at least some of its implications, may seem unpalatable; but it is incarnated in Mozart's major comic operas in examples of astonishing clarity and force. The imputation of such a view to Mozart, if unexplored in the critical literature, is at least not wholly new to it. Kierkegaard thought Mozart the most sinful composer of all;[5] and Charles Rosen has not only recognized 'shocking voluptuousness' as well as 'suffering and terror' in the composer's music, but has seen that these have been musically fused: 'the grief and the sensuality strengthen each other and end by becoming indivisible, indistinguishable one from the other.'[6]

Nowhere is this dialectic clearer and more elaborated than in *Don Giovanni*. While Giovanni must be condemned by the standards for which Mozart stood as a committed member of the Enlightenment, and *is* condemned by the socially progressive forces within the opera itself (for example by the class-conscious Masetto whose rebellious appearance in the opera reflects, as Katharine Thomson has pointed out, 'current unrest and the recent peasant insurrections'[7]), he is simultaneously the most dynamic and vitalizing person in the opera and its supreme and tragic hero. Giovanni is a socially destructive force at the same time that he is an energizing and quickening one: this is the opera's fundamental and disquieting paradox. To want a world with, on the one hand, the passion, love and forgiveness of an Elvira, and her capacity for change and growth, and, on the other hand, the sweetness of a Zerlina, is to affirm a world in which the 'diabolical' plays a powerful role. It had such a place in the dynamic and revolutionary world of Mozart's day – just as the interval of the tritone, the *diabolus* in one symbolization, underlay the thrustful tonal and harmonic system of the period while at the same time threatening it with its own negation. And the tritone does indeed play a prominent role, both thematically and harmonically, in *Don Giovanni* – a role signalled for it by the overture, through which it strides with a persistence and a defiance as shocking as that of the hero himself:

Only against this background does the climax of the opera achieve its full musical and dramatic significance. The Commendatore, entering at the end to denounce the diabolical, names the hero with a *perfect* fourth (commencing on the dominant) followed by an octave, and then fully enunciates the triad of D minor: thus for the first six bars he sings nothing but the notes of the D minor triad. He then completes his first sentence in the next two bars by adding only one new note – that of G, the subdominant in D minor. Tonal and moral – in a word, social – order are emphatically restored.

As Charles Rosen has noted, in concluding a meditation on *Don Giovanni*, Mozart's works 'are in many ways an assault upon the musical language that he helped to create: the powerful chromaticism comes near at moments to destroying the tonal clarity that was essential to the significance of his own forms.'[8] Another, and quite different, aspect of this linguistic assault may be discerned in the relationship between Giovanni's music and that of Anna and Elvira. Much of the women's music is in *seria* style: they are noble ladies who speak in the accents of a dying aristocratic world. Giovanni sings, of course, from within a more *buffo* tradition; as such, his musical style itself enacts the social dimensions of the assault to which his behaviour bears concrete witness, since his language – just as much as his profligacy – is both a product and a symbol of the Enlightenment, and of the Revolution to which it was giving birth.[9]

But the destroyer gives life. Negative though his role is, Giovanni is revealed as possessing a vigour and dynamism greater than that of any of the other characters. One manifestation of this is his ability to improvize. He is more adaptable, less predictable, than those around him, a quality that gives him extraordinary cunning in the most awkward of situations. And not for nothing does he have no real arias; instead he merely has three unusual 'set numbers' – the exceedingly brief Champagne song, and two impersonations. So far does he lack fixity or stasis – these being the very opposite of the quintessential 'life' that he is – that normal arias would be more than his mercurial nature would allow. Nor is it without significance that Giovanni is the only character in the opera to come into contact with all the others. For, as Alfred Schutz has written in the course of a profound essay on Mozart:

All the other characters in the opera receive their force from Don Giovanni. His life is the efficient principle for the life of all the others, his passion makes all the others move. It is echoed by the earnestness of the Commendatore, the ire of Elvira, the hatred of Anna, the gravity of Octavio, the anxiety of Zerlina, the confusion of Leporello. And all this is performed by musical means.

Take, as an example, Elvira's first scene. She stands in the foreground, Don Giovanni and Leporello in the background. The setting can be grasped by the eye of the beholder, the musical situation by his ear. But the unity of the situation is affected by the harmony of Don Giovanni's and Elvira's voices, and the beholder should see not Elvira and Don Giovanni together in the unity of a spatial situation. He should hear Don Giovanni in Elvira's singing.[10]

But there are of course varying degrees of contact—different types of relationship – between Giovanni and those around him. Some characters (above all Elvira) open themselves to his influence; others (above all Ottavio) uncomprehendingly shun him. These differing relationships are articulated musically: the closer the character is to Giovanni, the more deeply 'touched' by him, the more will his or her music approximate to that of the hero. Thus, in the words of Anna Amalie Abert:

as the only gentle character among Don Giovanni's enemies, [Don Ottavio] presents an absolute antithesis to the Don; a greater contrast than that between his arias and Don Giovanni's 'Fin ch'han dal vino' is inconceivable. There is, on the other hand, a certain affinity between this forceful song and Donna Elvira's 'Ah fuggi il traditor' (No. 8), in which she warns Zerlina against the Don. Her wild, seemingly breathless utterances paint a picture of the betrayer and at the same time of herself, a passionate woman who continues to love her faithless lover. The same holds true for the subsequently written aria, 'Mi tradi quell'alma ingrata' (No. 19c). . . . . He, in fact, sings more frequently with her than with any of the other characters opposing him – in the finales as well as in Nos. 3,9 and 15. In these pieces, too, he seems musically linked to or subtly attuned to her.[11] ٜ.6

Ottavio's antithesis to Giovanni is particularly striking. It is this very antithesis that throws light on Ottavio's fundamental sterility as a human being. Having no comprehension or acceptance of the darker side of things, he is resolutely and unthinkingly opposed to Giovanni. Appropriately, he is a tenor (bright, high), whereas Giovanni is a bass (dark, low). His limitations are revealed to us in our very first encounter with him, immediately after Giovanni has killed Anna's father. Ottavio meets Anna's grief with a mixture of bafflement and refusal. Essentially, his attitude is: Anna must not be allowed to see the body lest it distress her; and Anna must not grieve so much, must not even think about what has happened, as Ottavio will now be both father and husband to her. Mozart's setting of 'Lascia, o cara, la rimembranza amara' emphasizes the sheer banality and superficiality of Ottavio's sentiments. His kindly ineptitude on this occasion is typical of his manner throughout the entire opera.

In all important respects Giovanni and Ottavio stand at opposite poles. Giovanni sides with rebellion where Ottavio sides with the status quo; Giovanni symbolizes the killing of father-figures (in social and psychological terms[12]), Ottavio their maintenance (he will be Anna's father as well as her husband); Ottavio represents socially approved sexual relationships, entailing marriage and fidelity – an object he pursues with almost comic perseverance throughout the opera, while Giovanni attempts to subvert such safe, solid, society-building values. In short, Giovanni is life-ful because he so well understands tragedy; this is also why he is so sexually potent and so enchanting. Ottavio, by contrast, is a sterile character because he has so little understanding of tragedy; the likelihood is that he is also sterile sexually. Certainly, Anna's relationship with him is suspiciously passionless.

Negative and positive constitute a rich and life-giving dialectic in the person of Don Giovanni. Busoni noted that Giovanni was the man who gave every woman the supreme experience of happiness. What he offers Zerlina, for instance, is life itself. 'You were not created to be a peasant', he tells her in an utterance that also resonates with the revolutionary implications of the late eighteenth century's social philosophy; 'another fate awaits those roguish eyes...' And her music follows, and is enlivened by, his. Typically, Giovanni is a provider of feasts: wine, food, music, dancing, conviviality – all these symbolize, and are part of, the happier world that he promises. Charles Rosen[13] has rightly pointed out that the three orchestras in the dance scene symbolize the society as a whole, and that it is this scene that Giovanni *destroys;* but it is just as true – and another aspect of the living dialectic that Giovanni is

- that it is also he who has *created* this dance-scene in the first place. And Giovanni's potency lies also in what he creatively *reveals:* he reveals to his women the happiness to which they aspire but of which they are not aware until the moment that he reveals it; he reveals the unity of pain and joy; he reveals the importance of tragedy; he reveals to Leporello his own aspirations; he reveals the sterility of Ottavio. In this sense he is a stripper away of masks - and our second theme here makes contact with our first. Appropriately, Giovanni is also the world's most famous and most adept stripper-away of women's clothes.

Of the other operas under discussion, two were written after *Don Giovanni* and two before it; in all these, appearances of our second theme will be noted much more cursorily, both because the manifestations of the theme in *Don Giovanni* have had such extensive treatment, and because it anyway plays a lesser role in the remaining works. In *Cosi*, Don Alfonso appears to some extent as an aged Don Giovanni: like the younger man he is a savant about women, life, and the ways of the world; the motivating force in his opera, as Giovanni is in his own, he is nevertheless, like Giovanni, a cynic whose quest is a flagrant contradiction of many canonized values and beliefs. Despina is a related type of character. Possessed of an intuitive understanding - unlike her ladies - of the psychology of change so crucial to Enlightenment thought,[14] she inhabits with Alfonso the most socially progressive position in the opera; significantly, she is also the lowliest person in it. Her other attitudes follow suit: she has subversive feelings towards men (she talks of women ruling the earth), she lacks servility, and is generally reluctant to acquiesce in superstitious views of reality such as would belong to an older, and for her outdated, dispensation. In short, both she and Alfonso assume a 'creatively negative' posture towards the received social order, a dialectic that the 'lesson' of the opera most surely vindicates.

Cosi is quintessentially an opera of laughter: it eulogizes the act of laughing. Laughter is inscribed into the very contours and accents of its music - right from the overture, where the syncopated chords suggest reiterated belly-laughs. And here, too, we may discover a dialectic. During the overture – brisk, confident, in C major – we laugh *with* the established order of things, just as in the first scenes we laugh with the secure and solid Ferrando and Guglielmo against the impossible, outrageous threats of Alfonso. It is only later that we come to understand that ultimately the opera laughs not with but *against* the established order, as indeed we and the lovers join Alfonso in doing at the end: 'All four of you can laugh now', he says, 'as I have laughed and shall do again'. Emblematic of this change is the famous *larghetto* canon in the last finale, in which each member of the two couples begins to sing a toast to their future happiness. Slowly, and in turn, they enter with the same theme, but at the exact moment of Guglielmo's expected entry he sings, to a different melody, the words: 'Ah, how I wish that it was poisonous!' The denial of our expectations is sublimely comical; but now we laugh not with Guglielmo (as we did at the beginning) but at him, and indeed at the frustration of the canon's expectations that his wayward musical line has brought about. The subverting of the canon's expected order well symbolizes the opera's subversion of conventional social expectations: and the laughter that this musical joke arouses has not only the canon as its source and object, but the established social order itself. Retrospectively, we come to understand those 'laughing' chords of the overture in quite a new light.

A further manifestation of the dialectical theme in *Cosi* – and one first mentioned in our discussion of the theme of unmasking – is that it is the very *deception* of the lovers by Alfonso that liberates them from some of the illusions of their conventionality. Here the relatedness of the themes under review once again becomes apparent.

In *Die Zauberflöte,* good and evil, symbolized by opposing personages and realms, form the clearest and most basic polarities of the dialectic. We, like Tamino, are presented at the beginning of the opera with a 'world-view' that is to be inverted during its course. At first we take the Queen of the Night to be good, and Sarastro to be evil; later, as we grow in understanding, it is Sarastro who appears good and the Queen evil. But it is more than a simple inversion: the original polarity is also dialectically superseded, since Sarastro's realm is one which *accommodates,* in wholly integrated form, the darkness which the Queen so explicitly represents. His realm is not unequivocally bright: it knows pain and despair, and even regards encounters with death itself (most clearly in the trial by fire and water) as a necessary condition of enlightenment. Sarastro is clearly symbolized by light – and yet he stipulates a series of encounters with darkness as essential to initiation. This darkness has many forms, literal and symbolic: for example, a swoon, or a veil, or silence, or a confrontation with death.[15] And Sarastro himself (in his aria with chorus – No. 10) invokes not only Osiris, associated with the sun, the day, and the masculine, but also Isis, associated with the moon, the night, and the feminine. This duality of opposite but complementary principles occurs throughout the opera, finding true reconciliation – an integration of the negative on another level – only in Sarastro's realm.

In the works under discussion which antedate *Don Giovanni— Die Entführung* and *Figaro* – this 'operatic dialectic' exists in embryo only, and in forms that foreshadow some of its appearances in the later works. Commenting on *Die Entführung,* Brigid Brophy has noted that Constanze and Belmonte 'in their captivity. . . must make the journey through the darkness of death which Pamina and Tamino undertake at the initiation, and, like the initiates, Constanze and Belmonte emerge having vanquished the fear of death through the power of love.'[16] With regard to *Figaro,* one might concur with Kierkegaard in seeing Cherubino as Don Giovanni when he was a boy; and one might discern more than a mere outline of Giovanni in the character of the Count, who, as a dissolute and scheming lover, shares with him certain important characteristics. The comparison might perhaps be extended to include Basilio, the Count's assistant in his affairs, who thus foreshadows Leporello.

III

Mozart's concern with the ways in which human perceptions and actions can be masked, or mystified, and with the inescapable necessity of the negative for growthful social and individual life, speaks of an awareness of some of the concrete limitations, the imperfections – never static, and never to be taken for granted, but always to be surpassed and integrated – of human affairs. The conflicts, confusions, and falsities of such a world imply a condition that we might metaphorically speak of as a kind of 'woundedness' in people and in the social fabric that binds them. The third and final strand in Mozart's philosophy which we shall treat here, is one which refers to actions and inter-actions that give succour to these 'wounds' and finally heal them. It is the theme of reconciliation and forgiveness.

Die Entführung touches at important moments on this theme – most tellingly so at one of the central musical and dramatic moments of the opera, the quartet at the end of Act II in which the two pairs of lovers appear on the stage reunited for the first time. Most of the quartet's length is not taken up, as might have been the case with most other composers, with an expression of happiness at the reunion (though rightly and inevitably there is some of that); rather, it is mostly concerned with a harangue about fidelity – the men's suspicion of their women, the women's anger at this, and finally the men's pleas for, and the women's granting of, forgiveness. Significantly, the music Mozart provided for this quartet from the moment the reconciliation begins, until the end – a span which starts with the chorale-like A major Andantino, and takes in the plea for forgiveness by the men and its granting by the women – is among the most beautiful, and perhaps the most consistently sublime, in the entire opera. In another guise the theme of forgiveness recurs – but is only partially expatiated upon – at the end, when Selim sets his prisoners free and thus achieves the quality of 'greatness' for which everybody, except the unforgiving and hence ignoble Osmin, praises him. There is no mistaking the tenor of this moment. By his act of compassion he forgives a grave injustice done to him by his worst enemy, who is no less than Belmonte's father.

'It is far greater pleasure for me to right a suffered injustice through a good deed,' says Selim, 'than to repay wickedness in kind'. In tones only slightly more sacerdotal, Sarastro, in *Die Zauberflöte*, sings: 'Within these halls so holy/ Is vengeance all unknown/ And when a man is fallen/ By love is duty shown'. In his community, he tells Pamina, all sins are forgiven. At the end of the opera Tamino and Pamina, having endured their sacred trials, are united; at the end of *Figaro* the Count and the Countess, having endured their secular trials, are also reunited. Commentators have noted a fundamental similarity in the music Mozart wrote for these two occasions,[17] a similarity that is significant indeed. The completion of their purifications is the moment when Tamino and Pamina, having confronted and transcended the fear of death, find the veil lifted from their eyes; in *Figaro*, the reunion of the couple is the moment of confrontation and forgiveness, in which the Count is fully 'unmasked' and the pair encompass and transcend their recent suffering. The similarity of dramatic and emotional structure at the conclusion of each opera is thus underscored by the similarities in the music Mozart provides for each occasion. But the musical affinities enable us to see something of still greater importance: namely, the extraordinarily privileged position that forgiveness holds in Mozart's hierarchy of values, a position equal in nobility and sanctity to the purification and apotheosis celebrated at the end of *Die Zauberflöte*, and for which the reconciliation of the lovers is a reward.

Many other moments in which one person forgives another exist in our five operas: Elvira's forgiveness of Don Giovanni, and the reconciliation of the lovers at the end of *Cosi*, to cite only two instances. However, since their form is not essentially different from the examples we have already discussed, they will not be investigated here. It is more relevant to our purposes to recognize that for Mozart forgiveness may be important not only in relation to others, but also in relation to oneself. The most complex and suggestive instance of this is to be found in

Cosi fan tutte, in Fiordiligi's great aria 'Per pieta' and the accompanied recitative that precedes it.

The scene is that of Fiordiligi's second extended re-affirmation of her commitment to her betrothed and of her intention to remain faithful to him. In the aria she achieves something very like the status of a tragic heroine, the result of the collision in her of two contradictory sets of feelings – namely, honour and inclination, or in more immediate terms, fidelity and fickleness. But she is much more than a passive arena for these oppositions; her greatness at this moment derives from the fact that she openly acknowledges the conflict, squares up to it, and then, with all the honesty and purposefulness of which she is capable, chooses. At this moment self-aware, she is also now at her most profoundly human. This is why Mozart provides her with music of such range and beauty – though of course it is itself, through Mozart's music, that we come here to perceive her new stature. But one might infer that Mozart was impelled to fill these pages with music of such rare beauty because the dramatic situation touched here upon one of his most profound and abiding themes, that of forgiveness: Fiordiligi faces her own weakness, and in an act of truly human transcendence, accepts it and forgives herself. Human weakness and strength are here brought into inseparable and harmonious relationship; what makes this union possible is the forgiveness that Fiordiligi not merely asks of her absent betrothed, but implicitly bestows upon herself.

It is worth noting that all the themes of which we have spoken meet in this single aria. Fiordiligi here attains to knowledge of her true feelings, in their complexity: she strips away all masks. But these feelings present to her a glimpse of the 'negative', so drastically do they threaten her – and her society's – view of acceptable behaviour. In the process of discovering this 'negative', however, and indeed precisely because she finds it to be so real and deep a part of herself, she owns it fully and in so doing forgives herself.

IV

It remains for us briefly to locate the three philosophical themes we have discerned in Mozart's major operas within the socio-historic circumstances of the composer's time.

The image of a stripping away of masks is that of the act of debunking, the act of removing that which stands in the way of a lucid apprehension of a truth; it is the act, essentially, of *enlightenment*. As works that helped to strip away masks, Mozart's operas thus not only reflected, but also participated in the progressive social philosophy of the Enlightenment. One important and specific area affected, in an almost literal sense, by the act of unmasking, was people's assumptions about the supposedly 'natural' differences that divided and masked them. These differences had to be debunked, and people had to be revealed as fundamentally similar. In eighteenth-century comedy, from which tradition Mozart's operas partially spring, actors wearing masks are gradually replaced by actors without masks – a tendency incisively noted by Charles Rosen:

[In the seventeenth century] all men are different, each can be set off from his fellows, characterized by the abstract forces that govern his individual nature. The eighteenth-century view, by contrast, was a more levelling one: all people are the same, all dominated by the same motifs; cosi fan tutte: they all behave the same way. . . Eighteenth-century comedy springs from the tradition of masked players, but it made the mimes drop the masks as the century went on, as if the fixed grimace were irrelevant to the bolder, more mobile, real face underneath.[18]

Equally plain in its relationship to a wider context is our second and related philosophical theme: the negative. To negate is to subvert, to contradict, to unmask; handled dialectically, as Mozart does in his operas, to negate is to undermine the security of that which is, with the threat and the promise of that which might be. Such notions belong to the very structure of Mozart's thought because they constitute the very tissue of the historical epoch in which he lived, an epoch which found its emblem and culmination in the bourgeois democratic revolution.[19] The existence in Mozart's operas of a profound interdependence both of contradictions and their dialectical surpassing is thus to be understood as Mozart's creative reworking, in art, of those very principles as he perceived them and was himself fashioned by them in the particular historical conjunction that was the late eighteenth century.

What we have spoken of as the surpassing of contradictions is also, in one sense at least, an act of reconciliation. Thus our third philosophical theme – reconciliation and forgiveness – shares at root the same socio-historic basis as the second (itself linked inseparably to that of the first). More clearly than our second theme, however, the idea of reconciliation and forgiveness entered into the explicit – the consciously held – programme of the age. At a broad social level a great task of the time was seen to be the eradication of prejudice through the elimination of the religious hatreds and national grievances nourished by the clergy and the aristocracy. This objective, widely held by progressive men and women, was also the specific objective of the particular Freemasons' order which Mozart joined in 1784. Known as the *Illuminati,* the order had been founded in Bavaria some eight years earlier. The Illuminati differed from the pre-Illuminist Freemasons in that they gave up the idea of 'a kind of inner emigration, an oasis in which it was possible to escape from the prejudices and divisions of society at large'; instead, they

aspired to project their moral principles into society and thereby to transform it. At the end of the process there was the intoxicating vision of the universal brotherhood of man, transcending existing religious and national divisions.[20]

Forgiveness is merely a more personal form of this doctrine of reconciliation. And while forgiveness is of course a typically Christian concept, it achieved strikingly fresh relevance in the eighteenth century through the Masonic emphasis on reconciliation between people on the basis of equality.

The three themes we have discussed participate, in various ways and to differing degrees, in the essential substance of Mozart's five greatest comic operas. But Mozart articulated these themes in those works – and surely in others which we have not discussed here – not because he was attuned to some timeless or mystical process, but because, consciously or unconsciously, he aligned himself with the progressive social tendencies of his day.[†] That the five operas dealt with here are works of great and unique individuality is not in question; but that they singly and together are the concrete realization of Mozart's enlistment of his art in the cause of social progress, is a fact which fidelity to those works demands we recognize.

[†]contrary to Blume in MGG, ix

NOTES

1) *Music in London* 1890-94, Vol. III, London 1932, pp.202-3.

2) *The Don Juan Legend* (tr. and ed. D.G. Winter), Princeton University Press 1975, pp.49-50.

3) *Opera as Drama*, New York 1956, p.116.

4) *The Magic Flute, Masonic Opera*, trans. Herbert Weinstock (New York, 1971), p.84.

5) *Either/Or: A Fragment of Life*, trans. David F. and Lillian Marvin Swenson, I (Princeton, 1949), *passim*.

6) *The Classical Style* (New York, 1971), pp.324-25.

7) *The Masonic Thread in Mozart* (London, 1977), p. 121.

8) *Op. cit.*, p.325.

9) cf. Charles Rosen: 'The mixed genre in the eighteenth century is a sign of indecorum, and *Don Giovanni*, in more ways than one, is decidedly indecorous. . .' (*op. cit.*, p.322); 'The political ambience of *Don Giovanni* is given greater weight by the close relation in the eighteenth century between revolutionary thought and eroticism. . . . Political and sexual liberation were intimately connected in the 1780's (*ibid.*, p.323); and Brigid Brophy; '[In Mozart's opera Don Giovanni is] an enlightenment individualist asserting the Ego's right to pleasure against God, honour and society' (*Mozart the Dramatist*, London 1964, p.83).

10) 'Mozart and the Philosophers', in Alfred Schutz, *Collected Papers*, The Hague 1971, pp. 169-70.

11) 'The Operas of Mozart, in *New Oxford History of Music*, Vol. VII, London 1973, pp.156-7.

12) This point is carefully elaborated in Brigid Brophy, *op. cit.*, p.84.

13) *Op. cit.*, p.323.

14) For a succinct discussion of eighteenth-century psychological attitudes, see Rosen, *op. cit.*, pp.313-5.

15) A full discussion of the initiatory trials in *Die Zauberflöte* is to be found in Chailley, *op. cit.*

16) *Op. cit.*, p.209.

17) See R. B. Moberly, *Three Mozart Operas*, London 1967, p.143.

18) *Op. cit.*, p.313.

19) For a fuller discussion of the dialectic in its socio-historical grounding. its assumption into philosophy in the late eighteenth and nineteenth centuries, and its assimilation by the music of the time, see Christopher Ballantine, 'Beethoven, Hegel and Marx', *Music Review*, Vol. 33 No. 1, Feb. 1972, pp.34-46, reproduced in this book as Chapter II.

20) Ernst Wangermann, *The Austrian Achievement 1700-1800*, London 1973, pp.150f.

Chapter IV

Charles Ives and the Meaning of Quotation in Music

No MUSICAL style begins *ab ovo*. In the history of Western music, the emergence of a new style is marked by an incessant process of rupture, as each new piece simultaneously situates itself in an already-formed style and tears itself free of that style. The new piece is defined partly in terms of the distance it manages to put between itself and the stylistic type that characterizes it. To this extent, parody is fundamental to all art – indeed to all communication – since each new work of art must in some way follow established precedent. But although this is normally a 'simple' dialectical process, in that the new piece – the new style – is born from the womb of one immediately preceding it, this is not always the case. Sometimes the new piece will appropriate features of styles to which it is related only distantly or not at all. It is these stylistic leaps, the unheralded appearance of atavistic or exogenous traits as part of a new art work, that dramatically attract attention to themselves and raise questions that call for a systematic answer. The simplest and most basic of these questions is: What does the incorporation of these foreign elements *mean?*

This question has received scant attention from musicologists, and composers themselves have done little to illuminate it. Perhaps this lacuna is nowhere more noticeable than in the music of Charles Ives. It is to the particular consideration of this problem, as it occurs in Ives's music, that this chapter is primarily devoted. At the same time, the theoretical perspectives which evolve during the course of the chapter are sufficiently fundamental to have a range of application far wider than their immediate subject matter; it is therefore hoped that they will prove helpful in the understanding of the use of quotation and parody in the work of composers other than Ives.[1]

I

In Ives, previously existing music composed in a different (generally popular) style is introduced into a new composition for the sake of its *semantic connotations*. It is clear, however, that when a borrowed fragment is quoted it is not normally with the simple intention of evoking the fragment's original occasion – a barn dance, a circus parade, a church service – in all its erstwhile immediacy. The quotation is by no means an attempt by Ives merely to transcribe his aural experiences: an average New Englander of Ives's day would surely have found only a superficial correspondence between his and Ives's aural recollection of, say, the Fourth of July. But if literal transcription is not the point then manifestly some other purpose is being served. This purpose is the communication of an *attitude* toward that original occasion – a way not only of hearing but also of responding, feeling, relating, thinking – which is incarnated in the dialectic between, on the one hand, the fragment and the association it activates – its role as a *symbol* – and, on the other, the new musical context.

The general structure of this process is more complex than might at first appear and needs to be examined at some length from a theoretical point of view. In principle, the incorporation of borrowed material can take place anywhere along a continuum: at the one hypothetical extreme, the original meaning of the quotation can be unimpaired; at the other, the quotation can be totally stripped of its original meaning. Between these two extremes, an infinite variety of possibilities exists that always involves a complex dialectic between the quoted fragment, its new treatment, and its new context – that is, between (1) the original musical utterance, or 'linguistic act'; (2) the audition (reproduction) of that act; and (3) the utterance of the new composition. Since it is precisely the new setting that reproduces the original utterance – i.e. the treatment is itself part of the new context – for practical purposes categories (2) and (3) merge. This simplifies the process to a dialectic of two linguistic acts: that of the original, and that of the new composition. In fact, the new composition *is* precisely this dialectic.

Furthermore, for every quoted musical fragment in a piece, one can discover a process consisting formally of three aspects:

1) An extraneous fragment is 'chosen'.

2) A dialectic – which may include a distortion of the fragment – exists between the fragment, with its semantic associations, and the new musical context.

3) The new context has primacy over the fragment, by providing the structure through which the fragment, its associations, and its interrelations are to be understood.

For a model that is particularly helpful to an understanding of the structure and dynamics of this process, we might look to a realm far removed from that of ordinary musicological discourse: the theory of dreams and their symbols. While any full account of dream theory would have to differentiate between various schools of thought, for our purpose we need note only the following substantial areas of agreement:

1) The dreamer 'chooses' fragments of his past, which achieve symbolic import in the dream.

2) These fragments are 'never – not even when it seems so to us – a mere repetition of preceding experiences or events';[2] they have been distorted by such processes as (in Freudian terminology) 'condensation' and 'displacement', and as symbols connoting a wide field of associations they are woven into the fabric of the dream and establish the dialectic of the 'dream-text'.

3) The 'dream-text' has primacy over the symbols inasmuch as it organizes them and their relationships and provides the framework according to which 'the whole context surrounding the symbol is drawn into the question and examined'.[3]

The homology between this structure and that outlined previously in relation to musical quotation will be obvious.

We can assert, then (in relation to Ives, but clearly to other composers as well), the existence of some order of correspondence between a dream and a composition which quotes old materials. But one essential and fairly obvious difference is that the dream is private, whereas the composition is public. The correspondence between the dream and the composition certainly does not mean that there is a *simple* correspondence between dreamer and composer. If that were so, the affective sense of the composition would to a very large extent remain inaccessible to us. Rather, we shall need to postulate that a more real correspondence exists between dreamer and audience – where the term 'audience' comprises those who share, with each other and with the composer, a common world of meanings, significations, and associations. Of course, this distinction – that the dreamer corresponds to the audience (including the composer) and not *simply* to the composer – is not by any means a rigid one. There may inevitably be some associations and symbolic meanings in the composition accessible only to the composer; and there is always the possibility of a wholly 'private' composition. But these are matters which will be discussed at a later stage. Here our analogy can immediately be developed further. When an audience listens to a composition making use of parody or quotations from the 'public' realm, and when a composer writes such a piece, both audience and composer have the prerogative of *thinking about* the piece in an attempt to bring its insights into the rational and intellectual realm. At such times they assume the role of 'critics'. In our analogy, the interpretive and evaluative role of the *critic* in relation to the *composition-text* corresponds precisely to the interpretive and therapeutic role of the *analyst* in relation to the *dream-text*. And the composer's role has affinities with that of the analyst in another sense too. The dream is created passively, the composition actively – or rather through a mutual interplay of active and passive. This means (in the language of the dream) that the composer intervenes in the creation of his own 'dream' and, in doing so, he is composer-analyst.

These two basic processes – the creation and the interpretation of the dream-text, and the creation and interpretation of the composition-text – may in fact be more than simply analogous. In an important sense, they may perhaps be fundamentally identical; they may be the *same* process, but manifested in two dissimilar forms. If this is so, and if it is true that parody of some kind is fundamental to music itself, then we have another, and vitally important, basis for arguing for the healing power, the implications for growth, of music – or at any rate 'art music'. Dreams, we might say, tap the *private* unconscious (leaving aside the rather different question of the Jungian 'collective' unconscious); music (in varying degrees all the arts) taps the *social* unconscious. Dreams show the points of growth in the personal unconscious; music the points of growth in the social unconscious. Dreams deal with distortions in the person because of *repression;* music with distortions in society because of *oppression.* Dreams unmask the ideology of the individual; music unmasks the ideology of society.

Finally, if 'art music' is correctly perceived as the unmasking of social ideology, this may explain the significance of the incorporation of folk and popular melody (or its characteristics) in 'art music'. Its incorporation could reveal for bourgeois and aristocratic audiences the real foundations – musical and cultural – hidden by the distortions of their ideological everyday consciousness.

II

Two basic types of association should be distinguished: where the quoted musical material itself involves words (whether present or absent), and where it does not. Ives uses both techniques. As an instance of the latter, consider the last section of the final movement of his String Quartet No. 2. The previous movement is subtitled 'Arguments', and this final movement, 'The Call of the Mountains'. These final twenty-one measures are a beautiful example of a musical quotation fully in the service of a pregnant association. Situated in a 'visionary' D major with whole-tone-scale underpinnings (in the second violin and cello), they symbolize the regular peal of four giant carillons, one for each instrument. The image is made precise and particular by the quotation of 'Westminster Chimes' (formerly known as 'Cambridge Quarters') in the first violin:

Ex. 1

No cathedral city will ever *sound* like this heavenly evocation; but the purpose is not to suggest, programmatically, that having ascended the mountain the sound of bells is carried on the air to the heights from the valley below. Rather, this carillon image – unworldly though it is – is fraught with associations of majesty, awe, and revelation. The associative sound is now purified and intensified through its musical treatment as an *organized* polyphony of peals (in a rarefied D major) and is secularized through being sundered from its 'cathedral' setting and placed in a 'mountain' setting. This distortion of the image and the beatification of its associations – precisely *this* quotation of chiming – are what make Ives's point: which we might suggest (bearing in mind the 'musical disagreements' in the previous movement) by saying that the unity of man with his own kind, and the surpassing of the duality of man and nature, are to be perceived in terms of a privileged – indeed transcendental – moment of illumination such as that portrayed here in music.

A more succinct example is the general area of association which Ives appears to intend by his incorporation in the *Concord* Sonata of the four-note figure from Beethoven's Fifth Symphony. If, as we are bound to do, we take as highly relevant Ives's subtitle for the sonata – *Concord, Mass., 1840-1860*; if we also bear in mind that of the three Concord heroes commemorated in this sonata, Emerson and Thoreau in particular were passionate and articulate abolitionists, and that abolition itself was deeply ingrained in Ives's national heritage; then, as David Wooldridge has argued, the following association seems highly plausible: 'Beethoven's 5th = "Fate knocking at the door" = The Clenched Fist = Abolition'.[4]

The other associational technique (in which the quoted musical material *does* involve words) is also used by Ives. This technique was very frequently used by Bach, when he incorporated well-known Lutheran chorale melodies in his own compositions. The tunes would appear without words, or with a different text, but Bach could depend on his listeners to 'associate' the familiar words and thus discover a deeper significance in the work. If a listener does know the absent text of a quoted hymn tune or other word-associated melody, then the significance can be very rich indeed. An example is the quotation of the opening phrase of the hymn 'There is a fountain' at the end of Ives's song, 'West London'. Ives's piece is a setting of Matthew Arnold's sonnet about a London tramp's daughter who lets the haughty rich pass by, but begs from laboring men – 'sharers in a common fate'; the poem ends with the platitudinous optimism that the girl's spirit 'points us to a better time than ours'. Ives gives these final words a grand, even bombastic, setting in F major – but then concludes the song with a wordless F sharp major quotation from the beginning of Lowell Mason's hymn setting of William

Cowper's gory poem:

> There is a fountain fill'd with blood
> Drawn from Emanuel's veins;
> And sinners drench'd beneath its flood
> Lose all their guilty stains. . .

This musical quotation has the effect of subtly and ironically overthrowing Arnold's 'easy' optimism, since it connotes, by association back to the absent text, the idea of a purification by blood. And this ironic reversal is made especially forceful by virtue of the melodic similarity that exists between the bombastic culmination

Ex. 2

and the wordless fragment that immediately follows:

Ex. 3

Moreover, the bombastic phrase is itself a full flowering of the vocal line with which the song begins:

Ex. 4

Seen from this perspective, Ives's quotation – and the final perspective of the song – suggests: could we not have drawn this *difficult* (unpleasant, understated) implication from what came before, rather than the *easy* (platitudinous, overstated) one? But whatever the exact tenor of the irony, the essential theoretical issue is that none of the textual connotations of the fragment will have any significance for a listener not familiar with at least the opening words of the hymn.

In certain of Ives's works, it is possible to trace an intricate *web* of associations arising from an interplay of two or more quoted hymn tunes or other word-linked melodies. Ives's Fourth Symphony uses this as one of its associational techniques; a brief analysis of the first movement, the 'Prelude', will reveal something of the complexities of which this procedure is capable.

The opening of the work immediately presents a conflict: a passionate two-measure outburst on strings, piano, and trumpet – fiercely chromatic and destructive of tonal sense, and rhythmically complex – is contrasted immediately with a disguised fragment of Lowell Mason's 'Bethany', sounded very quietly by some of the prescribed 'distant choir' of two solo violins, solo viola, and harp, together with an *ad libitum* flute. The fragment is ephemeral, elusive, and fragile and after only one measure is submerged in the resumed passionate outburst. 'Bethany' (a hymn beginning 'Nearer my God to Thee. . .') is to play an important part in the work, a role that is vital to an understanding of the symphony; and its embryonic presence, in the third measure, is to be noted for more than simply establishing an immediate dynamic contrast with the rhetorical exordium. In fact the fragment hangs over most of the 'Prelude' statically, not developing or gaining in precision, and, according to Ives's instructions, 'scarcely to be heard, as faint sounds in the distance'; it is always played by the so-called 'distant choir'. But its symbolic function grows in definition during the movement.

The introduction of Mason's 'Watchman' (with an optional chorus to sing the words) clarifies the questioning nature of the movement and of the work as a whole. This Advent or Epiphany hymn is a dialogue between the Watchman and the Traveller, who inquires of the Watchman: '. . . tell us of the night,/What the signs of promise are. . . aught of joy or hope', and is assured, '. . . o'er yon mountain's height,/See that Glory-beaming star. . .!' Traveller, yes; it brings the day,/Promised day of Israel'. The playing through of this hymn reaches its most significant moment for the symphony at the Watchman's exhortation, 'Dost thou see its beauteous ray?' The several repetitions of this phrase are followed by moments during which nothing but the pervasive 'Bethany' fragment is faintly heard. The fragment thus clearly assumes the extra symbolic function of the 'Glory-beaming star' (in the precise meaning of the text) which brings the 'promised day of Israel' – the sign of promise sought by the Traveller in the night. It is this promise of joy or hope, still distant, small, and elusive like the star, that the symphony is to bring to fulfilment in the final movement. In this context the solo cello's rendering of 'In the Sweet By-and-By' (beginning in measure 5) is utterly appropriate; associatively we may recall its promise that

> There's a land that is fairer than day,
> And by faith we can see it afar,
> For the Father waits over the way,
> To prepare us a dwelling-place there.
>
> In the sweet by-and-by
> We shall meet on that beautiful shore. . . .

Moreover, the 'Watchman' tune brings with it a few accessories, the most notable being the first phrase of Sir Arthur Sullivan's 'Proprior Deo', which appears as a counterpoint. As another setting of the hymn text 'Nearer my God to Thee. . . ', its appearance here will emphasize, for those who know this verbal connection between it and 'Bethany', the desired identification between 'Watchman' and 'Bethany'; between the promise of the former and the fulfilment—though as yet unattained and elusive – of the latter. And its opening phrase is very closely related to the opening phrase of 'Bethany', which, though not explicitly stated, is nevertheless present by association with the Bethany fragment:

Ex. 5

III

Could one say that in the music of Ives there are moments when familiar fragments are incorporated, not for their uniquely particular associations, but simply as raw material woven into the fabric of the music? It is highly improbable that *none* of the extramusical associations of these fragments enters into the meaning of such a piece; in general, and at the very least, one has to insist that if the quotations are American (as they often are) some indeterminate connotation of American experience is intended or is at any rate inescapable. But it does seem to be the case that in Ives's *oeuvre* there are occasions – whole pieces or sections of pieces – when it is perhaps impossible to make associations beyond this very generalized level, or when associations are not called for. We shall return to this point later.

What is this generalized association, or web of associations? How one answers will surely vary from piece to piece. But in many works of this kind (even those where, for some quotations, more precise and particular associations are relevant), what is being symbolized seems to have much to do with the kaleidoscopic vigor of American life; with a notion that this vigor has its roots in the values of *popular* life (its communality, its fervor, its lack of sophistication, its authenticity); with an intuition that this life involves contradictions which, though at times tending towards chaos, must be affirmed before they can be transcended.

The 'Hawthorne' movement from the *Concord* Sonata may serve as an example of a piece in which the derived materials (stylistic parody as well as direct quotation) serve, *inter alia*, to connote a generalized American experience. Even without Ives's notes,[5] we understand the movement as a kind of fantasy. It is characterized by an incessant, crazy whirling motion, which gathers into its vortex a number of familiar derived images – ragtime, blues, march style, hymn style, patriotic melody ('Columbia, the Gem of the Ocean'). These images swim in and out of view as the music renders the world fantastic, with all the transience and the capacity to transmogrify its images that so uniquely characterize fantasy. The derived images tell us that this is Concord – or rather, American – experience,[6] but perceived through the distorting prism of a fantastic consciousness. Whether this is a child's consciousness (see Ives's notes in *Essays before a Sonata*), Hawthorne's, a drunken ragtime pianist's, a sleeper's or indeed ours seems not to matter. This remarkable movement leaves us wondering whether the (American) experience perceived through the fantastic distorting prism is real or unreal; whether what we perceive as distortion may not in fact give us a deeper, more realistic access to the truth than do the conventions of ordinary consciousness. Such a possibility is, after all, in keeping with what Santayana called the 'systematic subjectivism' of (Concord) Transcendentalist thought. The derived images, then, *locate* the experience for us by stamping it as American; they also act as norms by which we can readily comprehend the distortions wrought upon reality by the movement's own fantastic consciousness.

It seems that Ives also composed works in which it is difficult to *know* whether the quoted melodies are intended to carry any associations – or any associations beyond a generalized

American character. This difficulty will not be solved until an investigation has been made of these pieces, their quotations (provenance, popular usage, associated words), and the manner in which they use such borrowings. If this is so it suggests a 'secret' dimension to some of the music of Ives which can be revealed only by detective work. Or rather, it implies that such a work's 'secret' would be available only to an audience uniquely steeped in the musical 'folklore' which provided the sources for the melodies and styles quoted, referred to, or parodied, and that such an audience could understand the significance of the uses made of those materials – the dialectic between the source materials and their new context. Whether such an audience exists today, or ever existed, is a moot point. However, insofar as the borrowed materials belong to the public domain, the 'secret' of their usage by Ives is not *in* principle closed; it has the potential for opening itself in proportion to the listener's knowledge of the relevant sectors of the musical domain. Thus there is a continuum of intelligibility stretching from an 'open secret' at the one extreme to a 'closed secret' at the other, and for each listener any one of Ives's pieces using borrowed materials will have its place somewhere along that continuum.

For most of Ives's music of this kind, the point on the continuum designated for any work will vary from listener to listener; but there seem to be some pieces which for all listeners are near the 'closed secret' end of the continuum, and it is these pieces in particular that require investigation. Such research might prove that any one piece does not belong to the continuum at all, that *no* specific associations would seem to be intended or relevant. Alternatively, investigation might unlock a 'closed secret'. The first alternative, however, always leaves open the possiblility that any listener could bring his own private associations to the derived materials; the meaning of the piece for him would then be to some extent of his own making and would probably be different from the meaning constructed by any other listener. Such a possibility *always* exists for the music of Ives: whether Ives would have objected to that possibility or whether indeed his beliefs and his musical philosophy would actually have welcomed it are valid and important questions.

Ives's First Piano Sonata and his Second Symphony are examples of pieces on which such detective work might prove fruitful. Regarding the Second Symphony, for instance, we need to know whether or not some complex associational web of meanings is intended or relevant, stemming from the liberal use of quotations from Brahms's Second Symphony, Wagner's *Tristan und Isolde* and *Die Walküre*, Bach, Bruckner, Dvořák's the 'New World' Symphony, Beethoven's Fifth Symphony, as well as 'America, the Beautiful', 'Turkey in the Straw', 'Columbia, the Gem of the Ocean', 'Camptown Races', 'Bringing in the Sheaves', 'When I survey the Wondrous Cross', college songs, reveille, and various others.

On the other hand, there are cases where it is fairly obvious that we are not meant to infer the associations of quoted fragments – however familiar we might be with the original sources. The conclusion of the second movement ('Arguments') of Ives's String Quartet No. 2 is a case in point. At the climax of this movement, familiar themes are piled up with such rapidity that in the melee hardly anything more than instant *recognition* seems possible. In measures 90 and 91, the first and second violins quote from the third movement of Tchaikovsky's Sixth Symphony; in measures 94 and 95, the violas and cellos quote a fragment of 'Columbia, the Gem of the Ocean'; in measures 96 and 97, the second violin quotes the beginning of the 'Ode to Joy' theme; in measure 98, the first violin plays a few stressed notes of 'Marching through Georgia'. All but the first of these quotations is highlighted by the fact that the instruments introducing them interrupt their own rapid flow of sixteenth notes in order to play them; the sudden change in motion calls attention to the quotations in those voices. But surely the main point of this bombardment of borrowed fragments is not to create a dense interrelationship of associations, but rather to signify *incompatibility* – meaningfully so, in a movement entitled 'Arguments'. Each instrument is characterized to a certain extent in this movement: the second violin, for example, is rather recalcitrant, plays 'andante emasculata' cadenzas, obtrudes by means of stubborn, brusque chords. The incompatibility of the quotations coincides with – is indeed an aspect of – the incompatibility of the instruments, since the quotations are played by different instruments, or different combinations of them.

IV

So far my comments have outlined the problem, adumbrated a model by means of which the principles involved in musical quotation and association might be understood, and discussed the general question of the meaning of quoted materials in new compositional settings. It will be obvious, however, that meaning arises only in relation to a subject who constructs that meaning; it cannot therefore be taken for granted. Not only may the meaning of any piece be differently nuanced for each listener (a question of shades of interpretation), but different listeners will perceive meaning on different levels (a question of the *structure* of meaning). Three levels in this structure need now to be distinguished – each of which will, for the sake of clarity, be attributed to a different listener. Let us assume A, B, and C are listening to a piece using familiar quoted material. A concerns himself only with the 'musical' relationships in the work: for him the piece is abstract. B hears the musical relationships, but he also associates with the quotations, trying to establish their relevant connotations in order to decide what they mutually "say" in terms of the relationships that exist between them and their context. He may be assisted by some form of program written by the composer; he seeks the 'narrative' content of the work: for him the piece is program-matic. C hears the musical relationships, grasps the program, but knows that the meaning of the piece cannot be *reduced* to its program. Since he opens himself to the richest and fullest meaning of the work, he hears the piece 'musico-philosophically'. A consideration of two of Ives's better-known orchestral pieces will help to make these distinctions clearer and more concrete.

First, *Central Park in the Dark*. A brief description of this work in terms of our three levels of meaning would be as follows:

A. *Abstract.* The piece consists of a series of rich, flowing string harmonies, over which occur intermittent and fleeting appearances of other material – scraps of popular melody, fragments of ragtime, etc.

B. *Programmatic.* In Ives's own words:

... a portrait in sound of the sounds of nature and of happenings that men would hear, sitting on a bench in Central Park on a hot summer's night. The strings represent the night sounds and silent darkness – interrupted by the sounds from the Casino over the pond – of street singers coming up from the Circle, singing – in spots – the tunes of those days – of some 'night owls' from Healey's whistling the latest hit or the Freshman March – the occasional elevated, a street parade or a 'breakdown' in the distance – of newsboys crying 'uxtries', of pianolas having ragtime war in the apartment house 'over the garden wall', a street car and a street band join in the chorus – a fire engine – a cab horse runs away, lands 'over the fence, and out' – the wayfarers shout – again the darkness is heard – an echo over the pond.... [*Preface*]

C. *Musico-philosophical.* This level unites the others but goes beyond both. It regains contact with Level A, but negates abstract musicality in the direction of a more inclusive significance; it regains contact with Level B, but negates programmaticism by putting the narrative framework at a distance. At this level the imported fragments (e.g. ragtime) are not simply 'the life of people at this hour of the night in the vicinity of the park', but are part of a new and total fabric (the composition) that wrests another meaning from them. By thus seizing, distorting, truncating the quotations, by implanting them in its own fabric, the composition uses the associations connoted by those quotations, but implies an attitude towards them: it 'philosophizes' about them; more accurately, it uses those images as important building blocks, among others, in the construction of its 'philosophy'. At this level we think about (or rather we 'feel' or 'know') nature as the permanent ground of all human activities, utterly indifferent to such activities, but in a strange, paradoxical sense hospitable to them; we 'know' human life as rich, deeply felt, conflictual, but in search of happiness, transient and sporadic in relation to the 'empty' permanence of nature. We 'know' nature as unfeeling and unconscious – in philosophical language, *in itself* – and human life as feeling and conscious – *for itself.*

'Washington's Birthday' is the same kind of piece as *Central Park* from the point of view of its musical form (Level A): in it, quiet opening and closing sections, amelodic in character and of dense shifting textures, enclose a lively central section which consists of a somewhat chaotic mélange of quotations from popular melodies. This quotational section is longer than the corresponding section in *Central Park;* there we never leave the darkness of the park, while here (in terms of Ives's own program — i.e. Level B) we temporarily leave the mid-winter bleakness and join 'the barn dance at the Centre'—only to be returned after midnight to the 'grey bleakness of the February night'.[7] The reflective Level C is the dialectical synthesis and surpassing of the other two. Here we might contemplate the omnipresent 'winter' that encloses human existence, a winter of aloneness, emptiness, and old age; we might reflect upon the night from which we are thrust into the world and into which we again return; we might consider the notion of human community as a temporary haven offering warmth and a little refuge from the dangers that threaten it; we understand, indeed feel, the strength of this communality in its conflicts, joys, imperfections, nostalgia, and youthful vitality – the very qualities, to be sure, that give life to the central quotational section of the piece.

Obviously, the quotations of familiar themes in the central section add particularity and realism to the piece at the programmatic Level B. They conjure up a specific image of a village barn dance – not only the sound of the dance, its melodies, their inaccuracy in performance, and so forth, but also the rich fragrance of the associations that those melodies will have for (at least) most American audiences. But the meaning of these tunes is not confined to this Level B. The exact way in which they are combined, confused, *musically* treated (their significance at Level A) has profound reverberations at Level C. No barn dance sounds literally as Ives has depicted it here: this is confusion enhanced and redoubled – a musically *composed* confusion. Were Ives's purpose merely to depict a barn dance, he could have done it more simply and with less art. What is added to the simple, literal picture, then, is *art*: an enhancement. And this enhancement does not operate simply at the programmatic level, but rather is a *musical* characteristic (Level A) which unites with the *programmatic* intention (Level B) to yield a *musico-philosophical* significance (Level C). The enhanced barn dance *signifies* 'human community... offering warmth and a little refuge', and the other values discussed earlier. In the absence of such enhancement, the barn dance would have remained just that and nothing more; we might have *attached* these values to it, but they could not have been *signified* to our affective and intellectual understanding.

Could the musico-philosophical significance of these works have been conveyed without the use of those musical quotations? The question is important, for it is at the heart of numerous criticisms of the music of Ives. (Elliott Carter, for example, has said: 'It is to me disappointing that Ives too frequently was unable and unwilling to invent musical material that expressed his own vision authentically, instead of relying on the material of others.')[8] The precise and rigorous answer to our question must be No. Let us again use 'Washington's Birthday' as an example. Inasmuch as the musico-philosophical level is a synthesis of the abstract and the programmatic levels, we could not have known *precisely* what we know now – after hearing this piece – in any other way. Another piece (or version of this piece with the quotations replaced by original abstract music in an exuberant style) might have conveyed similar feelings and expressed a related kind of awareness – but certainly not this unique synthesis of particular associations (those dance melodies) with that newly composed music; that context for the barn dance, its telling embellishments and distortions, and so forth. We could know other, even perhaps related, knowledge and feelings by different (that is, unquoted) means; but without doubt we could not know precisely *this*.

Finally, it has been claimed that Ives chose all or some of his borrowed material for thematic and formal reasons.[9] His sketches for the 'Fourth of July', for instance, show that he was 'experimenting with the contrapuntal combination of "The Red, White and Blue" and "The Battle Hymn of the Republic"'. This led one commentator to infer that 'the melodic similarities undoubtedly influenced his decisions to combine these particular tunes'.[10] But one could as easily argue that Ives needed these tunes for their significance and he therefore sought for melodic similarities, possibilities of contrapuntal combination, and so on. In short, such claims cannot invalidate the possibility that when Ives used borrowed material he exploited it for his own connotative purpose. We should reckon with the likelihood that both criteria operate simultaneously – a notion that brings us back to our starting point: the analogy with the selection of symbols in dreams. For it is precisely the simultaneous operation of these criteria that governs the dreamer's choice. As Freud has shown:

If a dreamer has a choice open to him between a number of symbols, he will decide in favour of the one which is connected in its subject-matter with the rest of the material of his thoughts – which, that is to say, *has individual grounds for its acceptance in addition to the typical ones.*[11]

NOTES

1) Other composers who would seem to be likely candidates for similar treatment include (in differing degrees) Liszt, Bruckner, Mahler, Busoni, Debussy, Satie, *Les Six*, Stravinsky, Prokofiev, Shostakovitch, Janàček, Bartók, Martinu, Weill, Berg, Vaughan Williams, Tippett, Stockhausen, Berio, Maxwell Davies, Pousseur, and Penderecki. The net could be thrown even wider: one might also include the Gothic motet, Bob Dylan, and the Beatles.

2) Jolande Jacobi, *The Psychology of C. G. Jung*, trans. Ralph Manheim, 7th ed. (London 1968), p.74.

3) *Ibid.* p.90.

4) *Charles Ives: A Portrait* (London, 1975), p.305.

5) 'Hawthorne' in Ives, *Essays before a Sonata,* ed. Howard Boatwright (New York, 1961), e.g.: 'The substance of Hawthorne is so dripping wet with the supernatural, the phantasmal, the mystical. . . [This movement] is but an "extended fragment" trying to suggest some of his wilder, fantastical adventures into the half-childlike, half-fairylike phantasmal realm'.

6) It could not, in any too literal sense, be the experience of Concord, Mass., 1840-1860 – if only because one of the prominent derived images in the movement is ragtime, which came into being in its familiar form only towards the end of the century.

7) Ives's Postface to the score reads:

"Cold and Solitude" says Thoureau, "are friends of mine. Now is the time before the wind rises to go forth and see the snow on the trees."

'And there is at times a bleakness, without stir but penetrating, in a New England midwinter, which settles down grimly when the day closes over the broken-hills. In such a scene it is as though nature would but could not easily trace a certain beauty in the sombre landscape! — in the quiet but restless monotony! Would nature reflect the sternness of the Puritan's fibre or the self-sacrificing part of his ideals?

'The old folks sit "the clean winged hearth about,
    Shut in from all the world without,
    Content to let the north wind roar
    In a baffled rage at pane and door."

(Whittier)

'But to the younger generation, a winter holiday means action – and down through "Swamp hollow" and over the hill road they go, afoot or in sleighs, through the drifting snow, to the barn dance at the Centre. The village band of fiddles, fife and horn keep up n unending "break-down" medley, and the young folks "salute their partner and balance corners" till midnight;—as the party breaks up, the sentimental songs of those days are sung half in fun, half seriously, and with the inevitable "adieu to the ladies" the "social" gives way to the grey bleakness of the February night'.

8) Vivian Perlis, ed., *Charles Ives Remembered: An Oral History* (New Haven and London, 1974), p. 145.

9) See esp. Dennis Marshall, 'Charles Ives's Quotations: Manner or Substance?', *Perspectives of New Music,* VI/2 (Spring-Summer, 1968), pp.45-56.
   10)*Ibid.,* p.55.

11) *The Interpretation of Dreams,* trans. and ed. James Strachey (London, 1954), pp. 352-53 (my emphasis).

Chapter V

A Musical Triptych: The Contemporary Scene

A. ELITE MUSIC

SCHOENBERG SCOFFED at the idea of writing the kind of music that would appeal to the people he sourly referred to as 'the masses'. 'If it is art', he said, 'it is not for all, and if it is for all, it is not art'. We should not expect the most seminal composer of the twentieth century to have thought otherwise. Since the Renaissance, 'classical' music had been the preserve of a minority; and, in addition, art in the late bourgeois world was with increasing rigour refusing the socially accepted 'reality'. Today the trend is confirmed. Our so-called serious composers – and especially those of the avant-garde – write for an elite, and all those who do not understand their esoteric virtues – those 'masses' – are successfully excluded.

Contemporary music has fragmented into countless styles and idioms, both serious and popular, many of which seem to have no point of contact with the others. This reflects the atomization of society and is the logical result of our history. Music in the medieval world was homogeneous: the differences between plainsong, troubadour and folk styles were less important than their melodic interpenetration and their common relationship to a timeless, universal deity. But the spirit of individuality and dissent was latent within the integrated medieval secular styles, just as the seed of capitalism was

92

inherent in Venice and the other early city states that grew out of wealth plundered from the environment. By the time of the Renaissance there was a connoisseur's secular music.

Protestantism entrenched subjectivity. Science separated value from fact, and the rise of industrial capitalism drove a wedge between property and the forces of production. The Private Will came into being, insisting on the personal and the subjective rather than the public and the objective, turning intellectual against manual labour, divorcing work from leisure. The emancipation of the social subject – the Common Man – corresponds to the rise of musical subjectivity in the symphony and its homologous forms (sonata, concerto and so on), where the principle is that of themes (subjects) and keys in *opposition*. But this movement also made possible the emancipation of the composer from the hegemony of church and court patronage: he would now be a self-appointed, privately motivated artist working for himself (Mozart), or for a cause (Beethoven), even if this meant working against the socially received order (Wagner).

But further fragmentation was possible. The unity of Mozart's 'art' music and his entertainment music (there is no *essential* difference between his symphonies and his serenades) concealed an imminent conflict between subjective satisfaction and objective good. In less integrated men, the split had been more apparent for some time: the music of C.P.E. Bach often embodies both the style of bourgeois 'sensibility' and the bourgeois-popular style, while that of his younger brother, J.C. Bach, is bourgeois-popular music churned out against the author's better inclinations.

Music for art, and music for entertainment, were soon set on quite distinct courses. Poverty, loneliness, misunderstanding – even 'madness' – were now the possible lot of those composers who in choosing to be serious rejected the established standards of 'reality'. The last works of Mozart, Beethoven, Schubert – even Bach, in the *Art of Fugue* – are works written in isolation, often out of horror, addressed to nobody, or else private meditations offered up to an absent God or metaphysical audience. Entertainment music fell to vulgarity and commer-

sounds familiar

cialization in a decline that is easily traced through Rossini, Offenbach, Johann Strauss, Lehár, to Rodgers and Hammerstein and beyond. And in proportion as the general bourgeois taste declined, dragging the vernacular with it, serious musicians reacted by retreating ever further into a private, inviolate inner sanctum, and by inventing a language free from contamination.

It is against this background that Schoenberg's art-for-an-elite becomes intelligible – as does the work of the contemporary avant-garde, in this country most readily associated with the names of Stockhausen and Boulez.[†] Names – to most people little more: a bemused smile, perhaps an indifferent shrug. The first performance of Stravinsky's *Rite of Spring* in 1913 caused a furore; today new works by the avant-gardistes are greeted with holy approval by their tiny coterie of devotees. Those few who Know, approve; the rest keep away and do not seem to mind. The heirs to the tradition of progressive music lack an audience.

This shrinking of the appreciative minority until it becomes a group of specialists is new in our history. And it may indicate that 'classical' music has arrived – inevitably perhaps, in view of its history since the Renaissance – at a point of retreat where it no longer has even the possibility of ruffling, or grating against, the world if has refused. A paradox? Yes – and perhaps a good deal more.

The total rejection of a vernacular – a communally understood system of signs – is the most immediate aspect of the problem of the New Music. It accounts for the frequent complaint that this music is 'unintelligible'. But what is there to be understood? Certainly, there is little attempt at communication in any usual musical sense of that term: if the piece is concerned with its 'relationships', these are seldom aurally apprehensible, and seem only to exist in order to be grasped through analysis of the score. In the absence of a common language, and its potential for the incarnation of semantic content, structure and the systems that regulate it will be all.

Thus, too often, calculation replaces aural intuition as the way into the music. The specialists make pronouncements

† This article was written and first published in England in 1969.

about value as the only people who can know: 'You can't say it's not good until you've analyzed it', one of the young Stockhausen group in England has ruled. Music now mimics the prevailing world in which moral questions become technical problems susceptible of solution by the experts.

This technocratic tyranny has further consequences. A typical experience of the New Music is that, in the bewildering complexity of figuration, rhythm and metre are lost: the rapid succession of 'difficult' intervals means that frequently pitch seems contingent. Yet – as in much of the music of Boulez – the conductor gives the 'beat' with meticulous care, and the musicians generally play prescribed (notated) pitches. Thus rationality comes to seem irrational and, in a strict sense, incredible. This may be awe inspiring, but it is also mystification.

Nor does the New Music's own reaction against hyper-rationality, through the use of 'aleatoric' (chance) techniques during either composition or performance, suggest a real comprehension of, or answer to, these problems. For if the technocratic approach reproduces the world, randomization simply allows it to be. Both aim at fictions, the former at 'pure' objectivity, the latter at 'pure' subjectivity. The first eliminates the listener (subject), and then logically – since it tends towards a total self-developing system – the author (subject) as well. The second denies an object (the objective art-product), inventing it only to lose it in the environment: the event is a different and uniquely subjective one for each. Both approaches quite destroy the possibility of a shared experience, abandoning instead all participants in states of catatonic isolation. True realism, by contrast, would hold together these polarities dialectically as its minimum precondition.

Where do these trends terminate? Ultimately in two ends: in subservience to the machine (computer music is already with us), and in silence (like the well-known piece 'written' by John Cage for 4'33" of nothing).

But these ends are also logically arrived at by another trend in the New Music, namely its enormous complexity both of creation and reproduction. Soon, no mind will be able to calculate it, no hand or larynx execute it. That few enough can do this already, that it has rendered the amateur – and indeed many professionals – superfluous, that the required electronic hardware is beyond the financial resources or the highly specialized understanding of all but the most fortunate – all these are evidence of the hegemony of the new technocratic elite. By reducing the listener to a passive role, with no possibility of participation or comprehension, the New Music recreates the alienated state of his daily life.

Yet perhaps the predicament of avant-garde music is part of a necessary dialectic: freed from the need to make sense in the old way, this music establishes the precondition for the new sensibility. Sense – the old sense – must be emphatically negated if we are to live humanly and creatively with our technology – a precondition that the New Music, at least, with its invention of forms adequate to the restructuring of space and time, its extension of the raw materials and the techniques for the creation of music, and so on, competently fulfils. In the present non-sense of this music we may discover a truth: that avant-garde music makes no sense because we have not made sense of our technology.

And there may be a further dialectic here. If avant-garde music's necessary flight from sense has created a cultural vacuum, may we not expect another music to have rushed in to minister to the needs of the abandoned audience? I suggest that we may find this music, not in the conservative contemporary idiom of such people as Britten – who commonly founder in the false solution of preserving meaning by reverting to an earlier historical level – but in the best of rock.

Rapidly increasing the level of its sophistication, rock is vibrantly alive to the non-sense – and the potential sense – of the modern world. It is the first music to have humanized twentieth century technology. Its leaders – Dylan, the Beatles, the Stones – are the heroes of the young middle-class intelligentsia. They are a group who, with the ghetto population to whose musical idiom theirs bears a most siginificant relation, form the basis of what Marcuse has called 'the opposition in the centre of corporate capitalism'. The kinetic articulation of space through the dance their music gives rise to, like the idioms's potentiality for amateur participation, are a *praxis* that relates to the initiative of their vast rock festivals, and their agitation in – and outside of – the academies.

A genuine common culture can follow only a qualitative social change: this 'opposition', and its oppositional music, have surely a dynamic role to play here, now, and in the synthesis, later. The future of avant-garde music would seem to depend on its amenability to such a synthesis.

B. MUSIC TO FORGET

Within the confines of a tidy, solid box that is easily grasped in two hands, *Reader's Digest* has packed the following:

Eighty-four masterpieces of melody – the best-loved works of 50 composers. . . played by five great orchestras under ten distinguished conductors, a vocal quartet, a piano quartet, a nationally famous choir, and a world-famous chorus, and with, as guest artists, 18 top-of-the-bill soloists, vocal and instrumental, from Britain, Europe and America . . . on ten 12-inch high-fidelity long-playing records—playing time, nearly seven hours.

The purpose of the litany is, of course, not information but bewitchment. The music, like those who make it, is at this point anonymous. Nor need it be otherwise: for though it is doubtless the music – the records – that must be bought and paid for, it is not really the *music* that is being sold. Called *Music for You*, the record set is the latest in a series that has been offered in brochures through the post to a total of about six million people. Eric Robinson has compiled the programme of what would generally be thought of as popular classics; the selections comprise overtures, suites, excerpts, and independent pieces.

What is being sold is inseparable from how it is sold. Fundamentally, the publicity brochures hitch together two separate schemes in an association that bemuses the mind and senses. There is a lucky-number contest with prizes; and there are the records. At first the music· is not mentioned in the brochures: the news is that *Reader's Digest* has bestowed the stars in a beneficent configuration. Among millions, I am favoured – chosen to receive a 'mystery gift' in the Wheel of Fortune contest. And by claiming the proffered gift – which has nothing to do with the records – I miraculously become eligible for one of the major prizes: a Lotus Europa S2, three expensive colour television sets and four 'Holidays-Abroad-for-Two'.

Steadily, a universe is built up whose ways are quite inexplicable. Luck is its only law; yesterday I was poor, today Fortune mysteriously smiles upon me, next week I may again be poor. I am exhorted to 'make the most of my chances' by replying without delay: ten days is all I have before a fickle Fortune turns away her gaze. And in entering the contest, I cannot be held responsible for my failure – or my success. This is not a test: it is the purest affirmation of accident. Far from even being asked to guess the world sales of last year's *Reader's Digest,* I am required only to apply a lick of the tongue to my 'lucky number ticket', stick it and post it, when I claim my gift.

The record collection is at length less introduced than insinuated. After the initial warm-up, the brochure draws me aside to tell me about my 'privilege': the concept is crucial, for it validates the lucky-number principle by implicit analogy with the everyday world. The implication is this. If the world always seems to consist of a few who are 'privileged' and many who are not, this is because we inhabit an accidental universe. There is nothing we can do about that: but we would be fools not to 'make the most of our chances' when our lucky number comes up. And it is part of my present mysterious good fortune that I have this 'privilege': I can buy the 'once-in-a-lifetime' collection of *Music for You* – and at a reduced price.

Through association, the music – even before I know what it is – comes to be coloured by the allurements of the contest. The connection is confirmed by the nonverbal method of reply. I am presented with an order card containing an incomplete colour picture of the Lotus I stand to win. To complete the picture I must stick my lucky-number ticket to the order card; this will simultaneously enter me in the contest and bring me the records. Music, privilege and property thus fuse in the image of a Lotus Europa S2.

The whole offer grants access to the world of fame and 'high' culture, as much as to the world of wealth. They are indeed the same world, both being a function of my accidental 'privilege'. Money, as they say, has been no object: the musical directive, one is told, was 'simply to produce the best of everything', and I am plainly intended to be overwhelmed by the *quantity* of art and fame gathered into one place. The boundaries between the concrete and the insubstantial, between reality and fantasy, between life and a vicarious existence, have vanished altogether.

The process is clinched when the genie of the offering is rubbed into existence – the one in whom all images coalesce, the spirit who moves between earth and heaven, who unites the myths: Eric Robinson. After many years as a television host he is a known, familiar entity. As our personal guide to this accidentally magical universe – into it he 'has managed to put everything except his famous smile' – he is himself enchanted. He is our friend ('Eric'): but he also – *mirabile dictu!* – has 'so many' of his 'personal friends' among the galaxy of famous performers on the records.

Flesh and blood, he is a modest man, one of the people: 'You've no idea how humble it can make you feel', he will tell you diffidently, 'to have a cabby wave aside your fare and tell you: "It's a pleasure, Mr. Robinson".' Yet he is 'privileged': he is famous, rich and 'cultured'.

He has another function. He must assure us that we will like the music, if any of it should perforate the fabric of fiction, wish-fulfilment, illusion, flattery and comfort that surrounds it. His mere presence is a strong guarantee – his status as a known, safe and thoroughly dependable 'musical' factor. But lest anybody neurotically have any suspicions that a single traditional value will be disturbed by this set, a few personal details are sketched in.

For instance, our Eric is a family man. His proudest moment was when he presented his conductor-brother as a guest on his television programme, 'knowing that, at home, his father was watching'. Eric did wartime army service, in common with several of the performers, including the Master of the Queen's Musick who was mentioned in despatches.

Not safe enough yet. Not enough even that the selections comprise some of the most frequently played, broadcast and recorded music in existence, and some of the most accessible. The final coup suppresses the music by two means. First, by devaluing it. The pieces are all proffered as 'tunes'. Thus Bach is described as 'that very popular writer of hit tunes'. Now the precise nature of a tune is that it is infinitely abstractable. As it is unencumbered with considerations of formal context, it is easily 'arranged' (hence the many arrangements on this set). It doesn't *belong* anywhere: it is a multi-purpose commodity cheaply bought and cheaply sold, just one ingredient in a musical mixture. A tune is easy. It is what you whistle when you are thinking about something else. Hymns have tunes, some other kinds of group song (rugby, patriotic) have tunes. On the other hand, symphonies have 'themes', rock songs have a 'sound': these are *inseparable* from their totality. And in truth there are very few tunes on this set.

Second, the music is suppressed by obscuring it still further. There is an implicit attempt to give a predominant mood to each of the records, and the pieces are grouped so that they support that mood – or at any rate create the least possible friction with it. But each mood has less to do with the music itself than with its titles, less to do with the contexts from which it is torn than with the specious, preordained category into which it is coaxed. It is thus mainly one's predisposition that will ensure coherence to any disc, etched out in general by the broad associations of the 'privileged' universe, and now in particular by the seductive extra-musical details of each record – especially in its plush, alluring cover (also reproduced in the brochure). One cover features the last night at the Proms, with streamers: the mood of the album is patriotic pomp. Another pictures a half-opened Victorian jewel box in soft focus, and lists among its titles *Romance, Ave Maria* and *Valse Sentimentale.*

Passive mood has thus successfully deposed active imagination. If the loss is only of that kind of artistic engagement that potentially remakes both us and the world, *Reader's Digest* will not be disappointed: it is not desirable that at the moment the world should seem other than accidental; still less that anyone should think of remaking it.

C. *SAY IT STRAIGHT*†

Bob Dylan will be 30 next year. Young men may sometimes be old: at 30 Schubert was writing his maturest works and would be dead the following year, Mozart had just completed *Figaro* and had only six years to live. If Dylan had died of that motorcycle accident in 1966 in which he broke his neck, it would have seemed to us that he had always been old: that the tired, rusty voice labouring out of that beansprout frame bespoke the disillusionment of an entire era. But Dylan has lived to call for another judgment. His work since 1966 has asked – even explicitly – that we regard those earlier songs as the work of a *young* man, and that we take note of a man now wise and genuinely older.

Of course, everybody has heard about how much his work has changed. But it is more notorious than known. We have heard only the hubbub, and not the sounds. It now seems to me that these instant responses were wrong: that in leaping too eagerly at the tag 'Nixonian' to describe *Nashville Skyline* (released last year, the second of the two albums Dylan has made since his accident) we failed to spot a crucial moment of maturation in one of the authentic voices of our time and that we failed to detect in this change the arrival in rock music of a view of life that may, in a quite specific sence, be called tragic.

But we need to go back a little, to Dylan's five years of recording before 1966. In particular, there are the songs of

---

† This article was written and first published in 1970; it is explicitly addressed to what was then Bob Dylan's latest album, as well as to the latest album by his former group, The Band. No longer topical now in quite the way it was then, it may still be of some interest as an interim review of Dylan and The Band, as well as for its mode of approach.

incisive social criticism, and there are the love lyrics. The two are inseparable, even at their most distinct. Essentially, these are songs of loneliness in which Dylan's plaintive harmonica is the perfect symbol; his melodies, falling from a point of high tension at the beginning, are the stylisation of a cry.

If Dylan was alone, he was alone out of choice: the nightmare his songs so often relate is the world he had refused. He despised Them: self-consciously he tried to adopt a position on the outside. His rejection was always fierce, sometimes bitter. In a song called *I shall be free – No. 10,* he swore to grow his hair down to his feet, ride into the country club on a horse carrying the *New York Times,* and blow Their minds. Yet there seemed to be no way out: not even his love-relationships offered a haven. As one after another they came to resemble the dehumanizing game he had rejected, his voice grew to a frenzy.

Fundamental to this ethic of protest was the relegation of the alternative to the realm of the ideal. Dylan also wrote a few love songs of such gentleness that they respire with a quite incandescent beauty. They are addressed to no earthly woman, but to a goddess-like figure who is to be venerated only. Wearing an Egyptian ring that sparkles before she speaks, speaking like silence and in paradoxes, knowing too much to argue or to judge, associated with trumpet, Chinese flute and Arabian drum, even once described as an artist – she seems to be Dylan's muse. She has various guises. On *Blonde on Blonde,* the last album before the accident, she is probably at one point the Johanna who taunts him in visions while he is with an earthly women.

But there is something new in this collection. It is more than the redeeming sense of humour, sometimes at Dylan's own expense. (Perhaps after all it's a bit funny being stuck inside of Mobile with the Memphis blues again!). It is more also than the wit that can transform a bitter personal attack into a sharp satire. What is new above all is the attempt to *humanize* the goddess, to seek her among men, a flawed, vulnerable, suffering creature. *Sad-eyed Lady of the Lowlands* fuses religious fervour with a compassion and protectiveness that properly belongs to the human realm: she must now be defended against those who would abuse her, rape and destroy her. She is a madonna with a saint's face, holding the child of the hoodlum in her arms.

Here begins the abandonment of the false, utopian alternative that Dylan works out on *John Wesley Harding* (1968). The ascetic, allegorical tales that are told in this next album propose the view that a solution based on a flat rejection of that which is problematic is no solution at all. The answer is in the problem itself. Only the Joker can say 'there must be some way out of here' – like Frankie Lee, who died mistaking Paradise for that home across the road. The landlord is a fact; don't underestimate him. 'My dreams', sings Dylan, 'are beyond control'. The easy rejection was part of those dreams.

But then follows – of all things – a celebration. *Nashville Skyline* is that celebration; and it really begins on the last track of *John Wesley Harding*, with Dylan inviting his goddess, now fallen, to kick her shoes off. Meaningfully, it is a song called *I'll Be Your Baby Tonight.* And he celebrates for what he must affirm in spite of the dreams he has lost – or rather, *because* he has lost them.

The key to this is on *Nashville Skyline,* where in a kind of biographical review he sings, 'I never knew what I had until I threw it all away'. The song is sad without bitterness, wise without arrogance, remorseful without nostalgia. I think the way it has its roots in pain – the way it knows suffering, but most important speaks now, in the present, from a point beyond that suffering and with a sense of the preciousness of the values wrought out of suffering – I think these are qualities without precedent in rock music.

Of course rock, emerging from a blues tradition, has always been aware of pain, and Bob Dylan more than any; but it has never transcended its pain in quite this way. Is that surprising? Only pain endured is suffering, and only suffering transcended is wisdom: Dylan was twenty when he made his first album. Now wise, he would ask us to learn: 'Take a tip from one who tried', he says, and points the line with a gentle discord on the guitar that is more felt through the nerve endings than heard.

For reasons such as these, the simplicities of *Nashville Skyline* are deceptive. The songs are simple not because they deal in the trivial but because they have found, and mean to speak, the essential. Seldom has Dylan achieved such lyrical eloquence with such utterly simple means. But the result never sounds corny because it is consummately skilful, and because a complex emotion is always so clearly its necessary foundation: the past has had to be complex for this present to be so pure, for the musico-poetic statement to be so direct. Few people today can manage such forthrightness – say it so straight, and be simple without being trite. It is Dylan's new acceptance of a complex picture of reality, of a world with contradictions in which there is no gain without loss, that I would call his tragic awareness. It is a view of life, not a passing glance. Besides Dylan, its most articulate sponsor is the group called The Band, who on a rising tide of acclaim have recently released their second album: significantly, they have over many years had a close and formative association with Dylan.

Where The Band differ is in their appeal to an earlier America – to the experience of the old white agrarian communities of the south and midwest. This is not an idealism: merely a historical scenario for the tragic theme we found in Dylan. Here the conflict proceeds from the impact on the community of gross disruptive forces, natural or human. Existence is an unceasing struggle. The songs tell of hunger, cold, fire, drought, evil, the storm that's 'gonna blow this ole town away', Yankee violence, exploitation, change, decay, death. Suffering is a way of life, lived collectively; it yields and sharpens values, asserted communally.

Since solidarity and the capacity of the community to transcend suffering are among such values, these strophic songs make telling use of the chorus. Verses tend to be sung in a strained high tenor, with the solo singer dragging the beat as though on the verge of collapse; the communal choruses return like pillars, supporting the whole structure. All the voices bark and caw, and the band itself affects a rude, heavy, clanging-and-twanging sound: one hears the unremitting sheer plod, but also the relilience, of generations.

Simultaneous with Dylan's acceptance of the tragic is his switch from blues to country-and-western – basically also the idiom of The Band, though theirs is a complex amalgam. The switch has horrified many. But Dylan's adoption of the idiom traditionally associated with the most reactionary white sectors of American society – Nashville, Tennessee, is capital of the Bible Belt – is intrinsic to his new effort at confrontation. Country-and-western is the music with the broadest base in the white Americal proletariat; and the switch at least coincides with the current interest of the American left in relating to the white working class.

In this vernacular, Dylan gains a different system of signs, meanings, and associations. The marvel is what he does with this system – and the love-song convention that goes with it. He turns clichés on their heads: he parodies them, makes them ironic, even purifies them. The clichés are melodic (as in the nursery-rhyme simplicity); or verbal (with such rhymes as you/true/too, arms/charms); or instrumentational (as in the velvet caresses of a throbbing electric organ). At moments of tension he may suddenly leave such patterns. Just listen to the way phrases pile up in *Here with You*, until at breaking-point Dylan bursts the boundaries of the old phrase to sing 'I find it so difficult to leave', in measured triplets across the beat – an abandoned *parlando* line around a high dominant. It is a moment of lyrical genius. Though love songs, these are all public statements: here is another inversion. No music is more free of bedroom intimacy.

In fact, in the long series of night/day oppositions, for instance, night comes to be associated with the harmonious *social* order of moon and stars, whose light is in principle accessible to all; but since its light is also enlightenment, to be loveless is to be in darkness. The light of the day is a false light: day is alienating, divisive, offering a false sociability. The love songs on *Nashville Skyline* finally aspire to a condition in which society is not disunited.

Such control of irony is typical of the album. In *Tell Me that it isn't true*, a man worries about rumours that his girl has been unfaithful. Though he never says so, we suspect the rumours are false: the vapid syncopated interjections by the electric organ – another cliché – are a musical currency as cheap as the gossip which they suggest: and both they and the rumour's stereotype (that the other man is 'tall, dark, and handsome') are set off against the firm lines of the melody, its directness and honesty of feeling. Since it is the town that has been hawking the rumours, the piece also illustrates one way in which a love song may have a social concern as its true basis: it points to a wrong kind of society. Another example is *One more night*, in which a comic 'funky' style places the disappointment of a rejected lover in a perspective where it cannot be self-pitying, but becomes caricature through tongue-in-cheek self-parody. Grief strikes an attitude: the guitar *portamenti* are too much of a gesture, almost a flourish, the melody is too predictable, the tempo too bright. The hero becomes a clown, singing 'Oh it's shameful and it's sad, I lost the only pad I had'. His mask makes him Everyman, and like all clowns the object of our compassion. His misfortune is a social event.

It is a technique for disarming our sneer; but it is also part of a demand for an attitude to suffering – to reality – that would make the sneer an inadequate response. What Dylan calls for is not a flight to a romantic idyll, any more than what The Band require of us is a nostalgic escape to the past. The new demand in rock music is for an adult vision. Adults ought to listen.

Chapter VI

An Aesthetic of
Experimental Music

EXPERIMENTAL MUSIC patently lacks an articulate aesthetic.
Precisely this lack enabled a reviewer not long ago to denigrate
experimental music as 'a rather amateurish branch of
philosophy and comparative religion, as against a genuinely
musical movement'.[1] Paradoxically, the detractors of experimental music include those who speak from a left-wing
position. What makes this paradoxical is, as I hope to reveal,
that experimental music happens to have implications that
derive from, and support, such a position. One difficulty is that
these implications are not often expressed at the level of the
music's 'content'; and current evaluations of experimental
music show no awareness of the complexities of the arguments
put forward by such radical thinkers as Walter Benjamin,
Bertolt Brecht, and Theodor Adorno (among others), who have
dealt with the problems of commitment in art, of experiment,
and of an avant-garde. A knowledge of their work makes clear
that an aesthetic of experimental music could well begin by
attempting to situate the theory and practice of experimental
music within the framework of arguments advanced by these
writers. This essay is such a beginning.

I

Advances in modern technology have precipitated a crisis for

107

art, as for society, of such dimensions that our old notions of what constitutes art, how it should be made, and so on, are rapidly becoming, or have already become, obsolete. Among those who have recognized this is Paul Valéry:

> Our fine arts were developed, their types and uses were established, in times very different from the present, by men whose power of action upon things was insignificant in comparison with ours. But the amazing growth of our techniques, the adaptability and precision they have attained, the ideas and habits they are creating, make it a certainty that profound changes are impending in the ancient craft of the Beautiful. In all the arts there is a physical component which can no longer by considered or treated as it used to be, which cannot remain unaffected by our modern knowledge and power. For the last twenty years neither matter nor space nor time has been what it was from time immemorial. We must expect great innovations to transform the entire technique of the arts, thereby affecting artistic invention itself and perhaps even bringing about an amazing change in our very notion of art.[2]

Walter Benjamin placed this quotation at the head of his justly famous essay, first published in 1936, 'The Work of Art in the Age of Mechanical Reproduction'. Taking up Valéry's theme, Benjamin says that "under the present conditions of production' art has new developmental tendencies. These conditions 'brush aside a number of outmoded concepts, such as creativity and genius, eternal value and mystery'.[3] This much was recognized by certain musicians about the same time. Hanns Eisler attributed what he called 'the crisis of concert-hall music' to 'a form of production made obsolete and overtaken by new technical innovations'.[4] This music must therefore undergo a 'functional transformation': it must remove 'first, the dichotomy of performer and audience and, secondly, that of technical method and content'. (That the 'solution' of Eisler's own practice – to introduce 'the word' into concert music – left this music much as he had found it does not negate the acuity of his criticism.) A concrete and conscious attempt to provide an art adequate to the 'present conditions of production' was made by Brecht in his Epic Theater. Inasmuch as its forms corresponded to the new technical forms – cinema and radio (as will be shown later in this essay) – epic theater corresponded to the modern level of technology. But precisely the theoretical

backwardness of contemporary thought about new art –
analogous to that which now faces new music – made it
exceedingly difficult for epic theater to be accepted. This
backwardness could not accept epic theater on account of its
'closeness to real life'; meanwhile, said Benjamin, 'theory
languishes in the Babylonian exile of a praxis which has
nothing to do with the way we live. Thus, the values of an
operetta by Kolla lend themselves more readily to definition in
the approved language of aesthetics than those of a play by
Brecht'.[5] What its critics did not realize – or perhaps realized
and therefore resisted – was that because epic theater undermined the idea of theater as entertainment, it also undermined
them as critics: its criterion, Benjamin argued, is not the effect
on the nervous system but the degree to which 'the false and
deceptive totality called "audience" begins to disintegrate and
there is new space for the formation of separate parties within
it';[6] the critic was thereby deprived of any 'autonomous' system
of aesthetics on which to draw.

How then, more exactly, was such a work to be judged? It is
of no use whatsoever, said Benjamin, to consider a work of art
as a 'rigid, isolated object'. To ask of the work, 'does it have the
right tendency (or commitment)?' and 'is it also of high
quality?' is to pose as two conflicting questions what should
dialectically be posed as one. This can be done only if the work
is 'inserted into the context of living social relations'. Instead
of asking 'what is a work's position *vis-à-vis* the production
relations of its time?' one should ask: 'what is its position
within them?'[7] This question is addressed to a work's artistic
tendency (and thereby, Benjamin avers, to its quality as well);
but it is also addressed to the work's political tendency. Since it
concerns the function of a work within the artistic production
relations of its time, it is directly concerned with artistic
technique. Left-wing criticism that seeks in art an explicit
content is thus revealed as simplistic – and possibly ideological
too, for it applauds what Benjamin calls the idea of the artist as
well-wisher or patron, and forgets that his place 'in the class
struggle can only be determined, or better still chosen, on the
basis of his position within the production process'.[8] Thesis art

E

in any case, as Adorno has shown, is perfectly acceptable to the culture industry. Or, in Benjamin's words: 'we are confronted with the fact – of which there has been no shortage of proof in Germany over the last decade [9] – that the bourgeois apparatus of production and publication is capable of assimilating, indeed of propagating, an astonishing amount of revolutionary themes without ever seriously putting into question its own continued existence or that of the class which owns it'.[10]

A committed artist today will therefore 'never be concerned with products alone, but always, at the same time, with the means of production. In other words,' Benjamin continues, 'his products must possess an organizing function besides and before their character as finished works. And their organizational usefulness must on no account be confined to propagandistic use. Commitment alone will not do it'. Two things are meant by 'organizing function'. Firstly, they must be capable of instructing other writers in their production, and, secondly, they must improve the apparatus of production. What is meant by 'an improved apparatus'? 'This apparatus will be better, the more consumers it brings into contact with the production process – in short, the more readers or spectators it turns into collaborators'.[11]

II

Does experimental music show evidence of improving the apparatus of production? Certainly the notion of participation is deeply rooted in its ethic. Even when the passivity of the audience is not in fact transcended so that the audience participates actively in the creation of the music, experimental music will almost invariably point towards a situation in which such cocreation might be achieved. Participation is accepted in principle, if not always attained in fact. But a genuinely participatory music has of course frequently been achieved in experimental music. As many people can join in the performance of Max Neuhaus's *Telephone Access* and of his *Public Supply* as have telephones, or access to them. In the former, the caller dials a given number; the sounds or words he makes are modified electronically and fed back to him. However, obviously nothing but 'solos' are possible here. In the latter piece this limitation is overcome: the caller's sounds are mixed with those of other callers, modified, and then broadcast; a player within earshot of a radio can hear the composite sound to which he has contributed. Such pieces not only show how the media might be available for the purposes of active musical participation; they also demonstrate in a very direct way their social possibilities. 'Art', said Cage in 1967 in a comment that would aptly describe *Public Supply*, 'instead of being an object made by one person is a process set in motion by a group of people. Art's socialized. It isn't someone saying something, but people doing things, giving everyone (including those involved) the opportunity to have experience they would not otherwise have had'.[12]

Community music of a different kind is provided by the environmental compositions of Trevor Wishart and Friends, published in a collection called *Sun – Creativity and Environment*. In some of these pieces, all of which have been performed, music may be a carnival-like event made in a village community by its inhabitants and lasting perhaps several days. Local skills as well as local sound-producing materials or objects may be adopted for musical use. After attacking audience participation as normally too limited, Wishart writes:

The entire audience should, ideally, be an intrinsic part of the event from beginning to end, and when this is the case they cease to be mere audience and the event ceases to be a concert; they create the event, it is theirs, it is no longer done for them. They are no longer 'the public', divided off from the 'Artists' by an unquestionable act of God which caused some people to be born with a 'Creative Spark', an 'Artistic Gift', destined to amuse the vast hordes of the supposedly unimaginative. (What child was born without imagination?) They participate in a creative process, and in so doing perhaps realize the existence and/or importance of their own creative potential.[13]

Closer to a traditional concert situation, but negating it at every turn, is Frederic Rzewski's *Free Soup*. Here the audience, far

from being passive listeners, are asked to bring instruments and
to play with the 'performers', who are instructed to try 'to relate
to each other and to people and act as naturally and free as
possible, without the odious role-playing ceremony of
traditional concerts'. Rzewski's *Sound Pool* sets up an improvisation in which a wide variety of people may participate;
its most explicit restriction is that imposed on the *stronger*
players, who are required for the most part to 'do accom-
panying work, that is, help weaker players to sound better'.
Equally anti-elitist is the same composer's *Les Moutons de
Panurge*, which is 'for any number of musicians playing
melody instruments plus any number of non-musicians playing anything'. Some of Cornelius Cardew's music is among the
most brilliantly conceived attempts to provide music-making
opportunities for unskilled (as well as skilled) players. In
several 'Paragraphs' of *The Great Learning*, for instance, he
has composed for different levels of musical accomplishment as
an integral part of a thoroughly organized musical structure.
His Scratch Orchestra sanctioned such differences as part of a
performing body, without discrimination. In Michael
Nyman's description,

The Scratch Orchestra (singularly unsusceptible to definition though it was)
defined itself not through constitutions or the intentions of one composer,
but through the interests, idiosyncrasies, ideas, creativity of the group of
individuals, drawn from any number of walks of life, who made up the
orchestra. The Scratch Orchestra's (unwritten, unwritable) constitution was
one which allowed each person to be himself, in a democratic social
microcosm where (for a long time) the individual differences between people
could coexist quite happily, without apparently being reduced to a common
'constitutional' or organizational denominator, where a nominal 'star' (a
Cardew or a Tilbury) had no priority rights over the youngest, newest, most
inexperienced member.[14]

Such an arrangement, Cardew has commented, 'fosters communal activity, it breaks down the barrier between private and
group activity, between professional and amateur – it is a
means to sharing experience'.[15] The Scratch Orchestra
therefore was more than just a performing ensemble: it was an

experimental *community*, which entered into social, ethical, and aesthetic experiment on a communal scale.

These tendencies may still seem new and surprising in music; but they merely take up in a more modern form the changes noted by Benjamin and others forty years ago in some of the other arts. They constitute what Benjamin described as a vast melting-down process, 'in which many of the contrasts in terms of which we have been accustomed to think may lose their relevance'. This process 'not only destroys the conventional separation between genres, between writer and poet, scholar and popularizer, but . . . questions even the separation between author and reader'.[16] Film is one example: 'the newsreel offers everyone the opportunity to rise from passer-by to movie-extra'; as a consequence of this, 'any man might even find himself part of a work of art'. Thus in Russian films some of the players 'are not actors in our sense but people who portray *themselves*'.[17] (This process, says Benjamin, has been held back in capitalistic Western Europe.) Contemporary literature is subject to the same changes. The situation that existed for centuries, whereby 'a small number of writers were confronted by many thousands of readers', has been changing since the end of the last century:

With the increasing extension of the press, which kept placing new political, religious, scientific, professional, and local organs before the readers, an increasing number of readers became writers – at first, occasional ones. It began with the daily press opening to its readers space for 'letters to the editor'. And today there is hardly a gainfully employed European who could not, in principle, find an opportunity to publish somewhere or other comments on his work, grievances, documentary reports, or that sort of thing. Thus, the distinction between author and public is about to lose its basic character.[18]

Similar changes can be discerned in the theater, notably in the work of Brecht. Speaking of the didactic play, Benjamin notes: 'through the exceptional austerity of its apparatus, it facilitates and encourages the interchangeability of actors and audience, audience and actors. Every spectator can become one of the actors'.[19] Such sympathies are in keeping also with surrealism, which, although it transmutes the artist into a magician does not thereby separate him from other men. The poet, Breton said, walks 'in broad daylight' among ordinary men. The magic is within reach of all; everybody is blessed. 'Poetry', added Lautréamont, 'must be made by all, not by one'.[20]

For Brecht a further reason why changes in the (theatrical) apparatus of production were necessary was that art had become merchandise, and was therefore 'governed by the laws of mercantile trade'. 'At present,' he wrote around 1930, 'the apparati do not work for the general good; the means of production do not belong to the producer'.[21] The theater, as apparatus, is given 'absolute priority' over the plays. 'This apparatus resists all conversion to other purposes, by taking any play which it encounters and immediately changing it so that it no longer represents a foreign body within the apparatus – except at those points where it neutralizes itself'. Thus the theater's apparatus falsifies; for economic reasons 'it theatres it all down'.[22] Epic theater answers this assault by causing a 'battle between theatre and play', and so destroys the old apparatus. This is a transformation that corresponds to 'the whole radical transformation of the mentality of our time'.[23]

III

The Dadaists sacrificed market values by means of what Benjamin called the 'studied degradation of their material'. Through the conscious use of the unmarketable – trivia, obscenity – they achieved 'a relentless destruction of the aura of their creations'. Experimental music seeks to achieve this too, very often in a similar way. Benjamin traces the 'aura' of a traditional work of art to its ritual function: ritual – 'the location of its original use value' – is the basis of the unique quality of the 'authentic' in a work of art. In the Renaissance things began to change; the secular cult of beauty 'clearly showed that ritualistic basis in its decline and the first deep crisis which befell it'. The advent of photography, 'simultaneously with the rise of socialism', then posed a serious threat to the artistic aura, precisely because it attacked the possibility of authenticity at its root; in photography no one print can claim to be the uniquely authentic print. But the real crisis occurred only a century later. Now, 'for the first time in world history, mechanical reproduction emancipates the work of art from its parasitical dependence on ritual'.[24]

What social tendency provides the basis for this contemporary decay of the aura? Benjamin answers: 'the increasing significance of the masses in contemporary life'. The masses today want to 'bring things "closer" spatially and humanly. Thus is manifested in the field of perception what in the theoretical sphere is noticeable in the increasing importance of statistics. The adjustment of reality to the masses and of the masses to reality is a process of unlimited scope, as much for thinking as for perception'.[25] Precisely the same social basis underlies experimental music. It too, in principle and often in practice, destroys the aura of a work – not through reproduction but by situating the phenomenon of 'closeness' at the very root and as the very essence of the artwork. Gone are the notions of exclusiveness, of elitism, of a private code, of expertise, of the unique and permanent work of art, of 'creativity and genius, eternal value and mystery'. The musical work in principle becomes creatable by everyone through a revolution in the apparatus of musical production (which includes its language), just as the work of art becomes in principle possessable by everyone through a revolution in the apparatus of *re*production. To be sure, mechanical reproduction did not enter into musical art as early as it did into visual art; in the nineteenth-century music responded to the desire for availability and 'closeness' by developing ever larger resources of production in performance (grand opera, bigger orchestras). It is not until the development of sound recording that music undergoes a reproductive revolution, a change that culminates some time later in the emergence of composition onto magnetic tape: *musique concrète* and electronic music wholly defy aura and the notion of 'authenticity'. But meanwhile music was already on the way to meeting these challenges in another way – through the introduction of alea as a principle of performance, which in itself negates the possibility of a unique authenticity, an aura, in the work. Mechanical reproduction in painting guarantees an infinite number of *identical* prints (as does sound recording); alea guarantees an infinite number of *different* versions or realizations. Both make it impossible for an aura to attach to the final product.

The emancipation from ritual achieved by mechanical reproduction (of which Benjamin speaks) can be seen also in the dress worn by audiences at concerts of experimental music, and in the rejection by such music of the traditional concert hall. The distinctive, formal clothes that are conventionally worn at concerts of traditional music have been displaced. The new audiences by and large wear their ordinary, everyday dress to experimental music concerts: they observe no distinction between 'life' and 'art' – or, rather, the art is felt as bearing a close and necessary relationship to life, and this proximity is confirmed equally by the disappearance of the traditional distinction in dress and by the emigration of experimental music from the hallowed traditional performing area. The pulling down of the barrier of exclusiveness and ritual is of a piece with the investigation of life in art, of which Benjamin and Brecht speak.

In a vivid image Benjamin summed up the current trend towards the desacralization of art. 'The point at issue in the theatre today', he said,

concerns the filling-in of the orchestra pit. The abyss which separates the actors from the audience like the dead from the living, the abyss whose silence heightens the sublime in drama, whose resonance heightens the intoxication of opera, this abyss which, of all the elements of the stage, most indelibly bears the traces of its sacral origins, has lost its function.[26]

Nowhere is the desacralization of contemporary art clearer than in that experimental music which seeks out the unique peculiarities of individual human beings and allows these to dictate much of the shape and content of the piece – a process already prefigured at the very moment that a composer stops writing every detail of his notation and withdraws, conceding authorship (in the same measure as he withdraws) to the players. Such a piece is Alvin Lucier's *I Am Sitting in a Room,* which creatively *uses* Lucier's own speech impediment: a marked stutter. He reads the text; this is recorded, played back into the room, and rerecorded; the rerecording is then played back and recorded again – and so on. Slowly this process filters out the content of the original text and replaces it with the resonant frequencies of the room, in the distinctive rhythm of his original reading. Thus the speech impediment is transcended; it becomes precisely that which gives the music its interesting rhythmic quality. Lucier says that he is more interested in the smoothing-out of his impediment in the piece than in the exploration of the room-resonance. Another composition of his, *The Only Talking Machine of Its Kind in the World* – 'for any stutterer, stammerer, lisper, person with faulty or halting speech, regional dialect or foreign accent or any other anxious speaker who believes in the healing power of sound' – has a somewhat similar aim, achieved by different means.

The type of response demanded of an audience in most pieces of experimental music is another aspect of the process of 'filling in the orchestra pit'. More than for possibly any other Western music, an audience for experimental music is expected to respond *creatively*. A member of the audience is not faced with a pregiven distinction between foreground and background, with certain discrete and readily graspable musical 'facts', with a given and sensible structure, with clear and sanctified boundaries which define what one's attention should include or exclude. (Even if not all these features are absent, they are at any rate markedly less present than in traditional music.) Such situations provide exercises in perception, or new ways of seeing or hearing, and as such they are perfectly in keeping with Cage's statement about music not being an occasion for passivity:

Most people think that when they hear a piece of music, they're not doing anything but that something is being done to them. Now this is not true, and we must arrange everything, I believe, so that people realize that they themselves are doing it, and not that something is being done to them.[27]

IV

One of the central themes in experimental music is improviza-tion. And it is here that one sees so clearly the social aspect of experimental music, related both to the transformation of the music apparatus and to the desacralization of the musical work of art. Improvization makes cooperation and *social* behavior, in the best and highest senses, into an aesthetic matter. By transposing concrete social issues and values in this manner into the sphere of the aesthetic, the audience may gain practice at observing social norms, the performer may gain practice at behaving in social ways, but in a sphere free from the payoffs or the penalties that accompany asocial behavior in everyday life. Historically, all forms of group music-making reflect types of social behavior, kinds of social relationships, derived to a large extent from current social practice, but wrought in the artwork in a form considered to be an ideal form of actual practice. In a Mozart string quartet, for example, we have a series of relationships in an 'ideal' form, derived from current practice: however, the form of their derivation, as Adorno has shown, is that of a *negation* of that practice. Now the presence of the composer and of accepted, known 'rules' which govern all participants is itself part of that current practice, and speaks of a world in which rules and values can be agreed upon, at least among the class to whom the music is addressed. Improvized experimental music does in relation to *its* current social prac-tice what a Mozart quartet did to its own; but the absence of an omni-present and omniscient composer speaks now of a world in which the precise form of the negation of current practice must be *discovered*, in which there are few already-agreed-upon rules or values. Cornelius Cardew has spoken of those values that *can* be agreed upon in advance. He gives special place to self-discipline, which he sees as the

essential prerequisite for improvization. Discipline is not to be seen as the ability to conform to a rigid rule structure, but as the ability to work collectively with other people in a harmonious and fruitful way. Integrity, self-reliance, initiative, to be articulate (say, on an instrument) in a natural, direct way; these are the qualities necessary for improvization. Self-discipline is the necessary basis for the desired spontaneity, where everything that occurs is heard and responded to without the aid of arbitrarily controlled procedures and intellectual labour.[28]

To put this general argument in other terms: in traditional music, the musical language is predetermined to a very great extent; it is a *donnée* and to that extent a kind of 'fate'. In experimental music, on the other hand, the notion of this pregiven 'fate' is radically overthrown; the horizons of the musical language are established anew with each piece, or at any rate each performance.

If the significance of improvization in experimental music is that it is 'open' and without predesignation, without 'fate', then this privilege is made possible by the language of experimental (and much avant-garde) music: a language more empty of connotation, of grammar, than any musical language in the history of the West – and therefore more full of possibilities for significance to be vested in it. This absolute 'openness' explains why as a matter of principle anyone can enter into it; it also explains why the most remarkable and undreamt-of significance can arise out of the combination of the most apparently independent and disparate elements.

A musical experiment recently carried out at the University of Natal aptly demonstrates this point. Four musicians, all with experience in contemporary improvization, and all of whom had played together on previous occasions, undertook to perform a group improvization in circumstances where no player could hear any of the others: Each player, with his instrument(s), was closeted alone in a room remote from those of the other players; microphones and contact microphones fed the sound produced in each room to a small auditorium where the total sound was recorded on a four-channel tape recorder (one channel for each player) and simultaneously played to an audience through four independent loudspeakers. There were absolutely no guidelines for the improvization, except to play 'musically' and to attempt to 'commune' inaudibly with the other players; apart from this, the players had deliberately avoided discussing any thing beforehand (including the approximate length of the performance.) It was clearly an experiment – the outcome was unforeseeable, and three of the four players were sceptical in varying degrees. The performance ended spontaneously after seventy-five minutes, fifteen minutes after the first player had stopped. The audience – and the players, on hearing the playback – were amazed. The composite improvization was an unqualified success in musical terms: the musicians seemed unerringly to be playing *as a group,* responding to each other with what appeared to be uncanny sensitivity. That each single player had improvized well was not in doubt and not surprising; but that the playing of the four simultaneously made a 'piece' of such unfailing musical sense seemed to defy explanation. Subsequently, the tape recording of the event was subjected to further experimentation. The four individual channels were separated, and then rerecorded in various staggered ways: each single improvization starting one minute after the other, then another recording with a five-minute delay after each beginning, and so on. The discovery – in something approaching the natural-scientific sense – was that each new combination yielded fresh musical significance and continued to make good musical sense. The explanation, one had finally to conclude, lay in the nature of the idiom: precisely because the idiom was free of pregiven content it was more adaptable, more amenable to rearrangement, and more open to everchanging significance being vested in it, than any earlier Western music.

It is worthy of observation that experimental music's avoidance of predetermination and its search for a new language are two more respects in which its program echoes that of Dada. By means of a quotation from Apollinaire, Eluard (in his Dada phase) justified his experiments with language:

> O mouths, man is looking for a new language
> No grammarian can legislate.

In Dada, the interest in and search for new meanings and a new language to incarnate them went hand-in-hand with a belief in the importance of what Breton called 'objective chance', or what others might call coincidence. The same nexus precisely is found in experimental music: the meaning to be incarnated is not predetermined, not even its 'horizon' need be known in advance; but the *method* by which it is to come into being is one that frequently, indeed almost always, involves a fundamental engagement with chance.

V

The emptying of sounds of their significance, fully achieved in experimental music today, follows directly upon the tradition of Debussy, Schoenberg, Webern, and others, where sounds progressively lose their grammatical referential value, and become more empty and open. As such, experimental music fulfills Adorno's criterion that in a world where the accepted realms and procedures of meaning are administered, art must not aim at 'formal conceptual coherence', but rather 'suspend', by its 'mere appearance', the 'rigid co-ordination-system of those people who submit themselves to authoritarian rule'.[29] The function of art is defined dialectically, in terms of the negative: 'In the world of alien administration, the only adequate form in which works of art are received is as the communication of the incommunicable, the smashing of reified consciousness'.[30] Therefore, art (particularly, experimental music) is in revolt 'against positivist subordination of meaning'; it 'jolts signification'.[31]

Such 'jolts' – where the safe, taken-for-granted world is called into question – are created by other, more obvious means too. Cardew's *Memories of You* (1964) is an example. It is a piece for piano solo, but the piano merely defines the orbit of the action. Sounds are to be made, according to a specific notation, in the immediate vicinity of a grand piano; the nature of the sounds is not prescribed, so that the piece might well be performed without the piano ever being played. Thus the grand piano becomes virtually a mere reference point in the center of the performing area. The title is neatly ironic. Other examples were provided by the Scratch Orchestra's performances of 'popular classics'. The draft constitution of the orchestra, drawn up by Cardew in 1969, lists these classics as one of the group's basic sources of repertoire:

> *Popular Classics.* Only such works as are familiar to several members are eligible for this category. Particles of the selected works will be gathered in Appendix 1. A particle could be: a page of score, a page or more of the part for one instrument or voice, a page of an arrangement, a thematic analysis, a gramophone record, etc.
>
> The technique of performance is as follows: a qualified member plays the given particle, while the remaining players join in as best they can, playing along, contributing whatever they can recall of the work in question, filling the gaps of memory with improvised variational material. As is appropriate to the classics, avoid losing touch with the reading player (who may terminate the piece at his discretion), and strive to act concertedly rather than independently. These works should be programmed under their original titles.[32]

Such activities have much in common with Dada's 'violations' of sacrosanct works of art – the best known of which was Duchamps's addition of moustaches and a goatee to the *Mona Lisa*. And both these spring from a motive very similar to one of the motives underlying Brecht's epic theater: the alienation of the familiar. For alienation, says Brecht, 'is necessary to all understanding. When something seems the "most obvious thing in the world" it means that any attempt to understand it has been given up'.[33] The tyranny of the obvious must be attacked: 'what is "natural" must have the force of what is startling'. In this way uncritical submission and empathy on the part of the audience are prevented.

Such devices testify to an attitude to the audience entirely different from that manifested in previous art. There is now no attempt to dominate or manipulate an audience. The actor's idea of the audience, says Benjamin – and this applies equally to the performer's idea in experimental music – 'is essentially different from the animal-tamer's view of the beasts who inhabit his cage'. These are players 'for whom effect is not an end but a means'. Thus the audience becomes 'an assembly of interested persons' (rather than 'a collection of hypnotized test subjects'), the stage 'a convenient public exhibition area' (rather than 'the planks which signify the world'), and the text – again, alike for epic theater and experimental music – 'a grid on which, in the form of new formulations, the gains of that performance are marked' (rather than 'a basis of that performance').[34] In a performance of experimental music the audience is not insidiously drawn into the music for the sake of a profound emotional experience; indeed, the music inhibits precisely such a response. Rather, as in epic theater, the audience 'will quickly feel impelled to take up an attitude to what it sees'. In Brecht's words, 'once illusion is sacrificed to free discussion, and once the spectator, instead of being enabled to have an experience, is forced as it were to cast his vote; then a change has been launched which goes far beyond formal matters and begins for the first time to affect the theater's social function'.[35] The attitude of the audience for epic theater – and, if my hypothesis is correct, for experimental music as well – is one that Brecht characterized as that of 'smoking-and-watching'. It is an attitude that brings about 'a theatre full of experts, just as one has sporting arenas full of experts'.[36] But insofar as it rejects the 'direct impact' of Aristotelian aesthetics which 'flattens out all social and other distinctions between individuals', non-Aristotelian drama (and music) rejects the notion of 'a collective entity', a 'common humanity. . . created in the auditorium *for the duration of the entertainment*'. Non-Aristotelian drama (and music) 'is not interested in the establishment of such an entity'. In requiring its audience to take up an attitude, to cast its vote, 'it divides its audience'.[37] Such an audience will be at the opposite extreme from that stigmatized by Brecht in the following passage, however exaggerated his portrayal of it:

Most 'advanced' music nowadays is still written for the concert hall. A single glance at the audiences who attend concerts is enough to show how impossible it is to make any political or philosophical use of music that produces such effects. We see entire rows of human beings transported into a peculiar doped state, wholly passive, sunk without trace, seemingly in the grip of a severe poisoning attack. Their tense, congealed gaze shows that these people are the helpless and involuntary victims of the unchecked lurchings of their emotions. Trickles of sweat prove how such excesses exhaust them. The worst gangster film treats its audience more like thinking beings. Music is cast in the role of Fate. As the exceedingly complex, wholly unanalyzable fate of this period of the grisliest, most deliberate exploitation of man by man. Such music has nothing but purely culinary ambitions left. It seduces the listener into an enervating, because unproductive, act of enjoyment. No number of refinements can convince me that its social function is any different from that of the Broadway burlesques.[38]

If for Brecht such occasions were characterized by hypnosis rather than anything resembling autonomous thought, one of the ways he hoped to begin to rekindle thought was by means of laughter. 'Speaking more precisely', wrote Benjamin, 'spasms of the diaphragm generally offer better chances for thought than spasms of the soul'. Like experimental music, 'epic theatre is lavish only in the occasions it offers for laughter'.[39] One example of such humor in experimental music is LaMonte Young's *Piano Piece for David Tudor No. 1*, written in October, 1960:

Bring a bale of hay and a bucket of water onto the stage for the piano to eat and drink. The performer may then feed the piano or leave it to eat by itself. If the former, the piece is over after the piano has been fed. If the latter, it is over after the piano eats or decides not to.

VI

Heinz-Klaus Metzger has written:

the term 'experimental music', if it is to be given any . . . meaning, could refer only to music which by its own terms of reference is an experimental arrangement, and can therefore not foresee the results that will work out in performance.[40]

Experimental: the term itself suggests a music 'fit for the scientific age' – the condition Brecht required of theater. 'An act the outcome of which is unknown', Cage calls it. Cage also distinguishes this music from music which is 'a thing upon which attention is focused'. Experimental music requires something different: 'the attention moves towards the observation and audition of many things at once, including those that are environmental – becomes, that is, inclusive rather than exclusive'.[41] Some experimental music is aimed explicitly at discovery in almost the natural-scientific sense – for example, hearing the unhearable (Lucier's piece for the alpha rhythms of the brain), or discovering the inherent characteristics of a room or environment (Lucier's *Vespers,* and *I Am Sitting in a Room*). In *The Queen of the South* Lucier explores those sounds that are effective in making iron filings (or sugar or other granules) move on flat surfaces responsive to sound. The piece bears an acknowledgment to Hans Jenny, upon whose recent work it is evidently based; Lucier's piece for alpha rhythms *(Music for Solo Performer)* resulted, says Nyman, from the composer's 'contact with the work of physicist Edmond Dewan of the Air Force Cambridge Research Lab in Bedford, Massachusetts who was engaged in brainwave research in connection with flying'; and Lucier's *Quasimodo the Great Lover* reflects 'the recent research into the communication system of whales'.[42] A work such as LaMonte Young's *The Tortoise, His Dreams and Journeys* represents what Nyman calls 'a continuous practical research into certain psycho-acoustical phenomena'; or, as Young says, 'To my knowledge there have been no previous studies of the long-term effects of continuous periodic composite sound wave-forms on people'.[43] A quite different way in which improvization may be experimental is, as Cardew has pointed out, its search for sounds that operate subliminally rather than at a manifest cultural level, and its investigation of the emotions that are stirred by such sounds.

The scientific frame of mind of 'what can we discover?' is thus one of the central irreducible features of experimental music. The active experience of this attitude is what cannot be captured on a phonograph record, which therefore has 'no more value than a postcard' (Cage). Such a frame of mind is totally future-oriented: its sole intention is to produce – in an attitude of open-minded, open-ended discovery – the *future*. By comparison, Western traditional music tells us what is, or has been, known or hoped or felt; its performances reproduce the *past*.

The scientific attitude evinced here is not new to twentieth-century art. Benjamin applauded film because it promoted the mutual penetration of art and science, and noted: 'it is difficult to say which is more fascinating, its artistic value or its value for science'. Its capacity for discovery was to be located in two closely related areas. Firstly, by the use of such techniques as the close-up, or the focus on details that may be hidden from ordinary view, film 'extends our comprehension of the necessities which rule over our lives'. Secondly, by means of slow motion, its capacity for infinite mobility, its 'dynamite of the tenth of a second', film burst asunder the prison world in which we appeared to be hopelessly locked. Experimental music does precisely the same. The microphone, contact-microphone, amplifier, tape recorder, and shortwave radio have extended our comprehension and freed us from our auditory prison world in an exactly analogous way. If the camera 'introduces us to unconscious optics as does psychoanalysis to unconscious impulses',[44] then the techniques of experimental music introduce us to unconscious sound production and hearing. Dziga Vertov's marvelous homage to the camera in his manifesto printed in the magazine *LEF* in 1923 could stand, *mutatis mutandis*, as a homage to the microphone:

I am an eye. I am a mechanical eye. I, the machine, show you a world the way only I can see it. I free myself for today and forever from human immobility. I am in constant movement. I approach and pull away from objects. I creep under them. I move alongside a running horse's mouth. I cut into a crowd in full speed. I run in front of running soldiers. I turn over on my back. I soar with an aeroplane. I fall and rise with the falling and rising bodies. This is I, the machine, manoeuvring in the chaotic movements, recording one movement after another in the most complex combinations. Freed from the obligation of shooting 16 to 17 frames per second, freed from the boundaries of time and space, I co-ordinate any and all points of the universe, wherever I want them to be. My way leads towards the creation of a fresh perception of the world. Thus I explain in a new way the world unknown to you.

For Brecht, a scientific spirit of investigation had to be one of the essential attributes of art in the twentieth century:

I must say that I do need the sciences. I have to admit that I look askance at all sorts of people who I know do not operate on the level of scientific understanding: that is to say, who sing as the birds sing, or as people imagine the birds to sing. I don't mean by that that I would reject a charming poem about the taste of fried fish or the delights of a boating party just because the writer had not studied gastronomy or navigation. But in my view the great and complicated things that go on in the world cannot be adequately recognized by people who do not use every possible aid to understanding.[45]

Galileo, Brecht reminds us, saw a swinging chandelier; 'he was amazed by this pendulum in motion', and his amazement was precisely what enabled him to arrive at an understanding of the laws that governed its movement. This 'detached eye', according to Brecht, is what theater audiences must develop; it is the job of the playwright to put them in situations where this attitude is required of them.[46] In a piece composed in 1968 Steve Reich requires his audience to observe *and listen to* a number of pendulums in motion. Microphones are suspended above loudspeakers, released simultaneously, and allowed to swing at their own speed. They feed back through the speakers. The piece consists of a changing series of feedback pulses, shorter at the beginning and longer at the end when the mikes swing more slowly: the piece ends with unbroken feedback when all the mikes are at rest.

Brecht suggests that people today want 'rational' entertainment – what Benjamin called the 'dramatic laboratory' – because of 'the whole radical transformation of the mentality of our time'. What is certain, he says, is that

the present-day world can only be described to present-day people if it is described as capable of transformation. People of the present day value questions on account of their answers. They are interested in events and situations in face of which they can do something. . . . In an age whose science is in a position to change nature to such an extent as to make the world seem almost habitable, man can no longer describe man as a victim, the object of a fixed but unknown environment. It is scarcely possible to conceive of the laws of motion if one looks at them from a tennis ball's point of view.[47]

VII

Benjamin noted the existence of a profound dialectic in the development of art:

> One of the foremost tasks of art has always been the creation of a demand which could be fully satisfied only later. The history of every art form shows critical epochs in which a certain art form aspires to effects which could be fully obtained only with a changed technical standard, that is to say, in a new art form. The extravagances and crudities of art which thus appear, particularly in the so-called decadent epochs, actually arise from the nucleus of its richest historical energies. In recent years, such barbarisms were abundant in Dadaism. It is only now that its impulse becomes discernible: Dadaism attempted to create by pictorial – and literary – means the effects which the public today seeks in the film.[48]

This dialectic precisely defines the relationship between experimental and avant-garde music: not a fruitless opposition but a fertile and changing interplay between the more and the less radical, the more and the less systematized. The two are complementary – indeed, possibly of necessity; one might ask whether either could exist in its familiar form without the other. And this connection points to their relationship to the modern world: they are the twin parts of what we might designate a quasi-scientific practice. In other words, the one experiments, the other adopts; the latter has implications ('hypotheses') which the former explores (subjects to experiment).

If audience participation entered composition haphazardly and unpredictably in Cage's music (for example), then in an avant-garde work such as *Momente* Stockhausen has composed this into the piece as an integral and predetermined part of the structure. Even though here it is not an actual audience that participates, the link between the experiments of, say, Cage and *Momente* is nevertheless valid. A more precise instance of experimental music influencing avant-garde music is that of Stockhausen's contact with David Tudor. Their acquaintance helped the composer formulate a new attitude to the role of the interpreter in his own composed music – an attitude which Tudor was able to impart because of his own deep involvement in American experimental music which viewed the performer in this way. For Tudor, as Karl Wörner has pointed out, was not so much a 'performer' as a 'partner', less an executant than a creative accomplice. As such, he was quite different from Stockhausen's ideal type of interpreter, who would perform an unambiguous score in the prescribed, 'correct' way. As a result of their encounters, Stockhausen came to see that a more 'open' attitude towards the score and a freer rein for the interpreter could achieve the decisive step of reinvesting the performer with some of the responsibilities of creation. Around this time (1954/55) Stockhausen began writing works that embody this new attitude.

But avant-garde music also provides aspects for experimental music to contradict. The music of the avant-garde, in its purest or most 'classical' manifestation, is still exclusive in its skill orientation, still elitist, whereas experimental music is, both in principle and often in practice, inclusive and participatory. This difference is manifested also in the different social status of the two musics: Boulez is performed at the Royal Festival Hall, Cardew in Ealing Town Hall; journals devoted to the avant-garde (e.g., *Perspectives of New Music*) are academic in a conventional sense, those devoted to experimental music (e.g., *Source)* are iconoclastic and may even be antiacademic in tendency; avant-garde composers tend to be respected 'establishment' figures, while experimental composers are, if anything, members of the 'antiestablishment'.

Perhaps more than any other contemporary composer, Stockhausen exists at the point where the dialectic between experimental and avant-garde music becomes manifest; it is in him, more obviously than anywhere else, that these diverse approaches converge. This alone would seem to suggest his remarkable significance. Of Boulez, Stockhausen has said: 'His objective is the work of art, mine is rather its workings'. And of

Cage: 'A composer who draws attention to himself more by his actions than by his productions'.[49] Thus the following polarity of extremes and their confluence emerges:

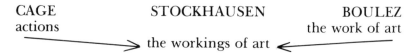

CAGE   STOCKHAUSEN   BOULEZ
actions   the work of art
                    ⟶ the workings of art ⟵

It is worth stressing that the underlying unity of these extremes is not in question and is after all what makes the dialectic possible. This unity is summed up in Morton Feldman's recent observations:

> What music rhapsodizes in today's 'cool' language, is its own construction. The fact that men like Boulez and Cage represent opposite extremes of modern methodology is not what is interesting. What is interesting is their similarity. In the music of both men, things are exactly what they are – no more, no less. In the music of both men, what is heard is indistinguishable from its process. In fact, process itself might be called the Zeitgeist of our age. The duality of precise means creating indeterminate emotions is now associated only with the past.[50]

VIII

The episodic character of experimental music and avant-garde music ('moment form' for example) has often been noted. In this respect, too, music corresponds to the new technical forms: cinema, radio, television, and the press. And this is one further feature it shares with epic theater. The connection between Brecht's theater and the new technical forms was sketched by Benjamin:

> In film, the theory has become more and more accepted that the audience should be able to 'come in ' at any point, that complicated plot developments should be avoided and that each part, besides the value it has for the whole, should also possess its own episodic value. For radio, with its public which can freely switch on or off at any moment, this becomes a strict necessity. Epic theatre introduces the same practice on the stage. For epic theatre, as a matter of principle, there is no such thing as a latecomer.[51]

Advanced literature in the twentieth century has also been episodic. Significantly, *Ulysses* was one of Brecht's favorite books. Michel Butor admitted that he had never read *Finnegan's Wake* right through; he claimed that an episodic approach to the book was the correct approach, because one had to collaborate with the text by reconstituting it for oneself, uniquely. 'The aesthetic object', Eduardo Sanguineti comments, 'is no longer a complete thing which is placed in front of the spectator'.[52]

IX

If some experimental situations are trivial or patently absurd, this may not necessarily be a bad thing, especially if one views them as *experimental* occasions. It is part of a scientific frame of mind to realize that experiments may fail or be inappropriate, and that there is something to be learned from these failures. And if one views the relationship between experimental and avant-garde music as symbiotic, then such failures may actually be necessary and inevitable in the development of a healthy and creative modern musical culture. Besides, frequent involvement with the progressive (questioning, socializing) aspects of experimental music may inculcate desirable new habits of perception, expectation, and response in audiences. To claim this is no more than Benjamin claimed in arguing for the importance of film *despite* its frequently trivial content. Film, par excellence (he maintained), has deveopled new habits in audiences, and these habits amount to a change in perception. The audience on a mass scale now participates; the aura has been wiped out; and members of the audience now habitually see themselves and their relationships to each other and to the artwork in a new way. This could not have been achieved by contemplation alone. Therefore we should not be concerned if much film content is disreputable. For film abolishes cult value and inaugurates the era in which the audience is at once final critic and true coauthor.[5] The very same is true of experimental music.

NOTES

1) Richard Middleton in *Music and Letters,* LVI/1 (January, 1975), 85-86.

2) Valéry, 'The Conquest of Ubiquity', *Aesthetics,* trans. Ralph Mannheim (New York, 1964), p.225. The essay was first published in 1928.

3) 'The Work of Art in the Age of Mechanical Reproduction', in Benjamin, *Illuminations,* trans. Harry Zohn (London, 1970), p.220.

4) Quoted in Benjamin, 'The Author as Producer', *Understanding Brecht,* trans. Anna Bostock (London, 1973), p.96.

5) 'What Is Epic Theatre?' first version, *Understanding Brecht,* p.3.

6) *Ibid.,* p.10.

7) 'The Author as Producer', p.87.

8) *Ibid.,* p.93.

9) Benjamin wrote this paper during the thirties.

10) 'The Author as Producer', p.94.

11) *Ibid.,* p.98.

12) Cage, 'Diary: How to Improve the World (You Will Only Make Matters Worse), Continued 1967', *A Year from Monday* (London, 1968), p.151.

13) Wishart, *Sun – Creativity and Environment* (London, 1974), p.8.

14) Nyman, *Experimental Music: Cage and Beyond* (London, 1974), p.114.

15) Cardew, ed., *Scratch Music* (London, 1972), p.16.

16) 'The Author as Producer', pp.89-90.

17) 'The Work of Art', p.233.

18) *Ibid.,* p.234.

19) 'What Is Epic Theatre?' second version. *Understanding Brecht,* p.20.

20) Quoted in Maurice Nadeau, *The History of Surrealism,* trans. Richard Howard (Harmondsworth, Middlesex, 1973), p.52.

21) 'The Modern Theatre Is the Epic Theatre', *Brecht on Theatre,* ed. and trans. John Willett (New York, 1964), p.35.

22) 'The Literarization of the Theatre', *Brecht on Theatre,* p.43.

23) 'The Epic Theatre and Its Difficulties', *Brecht on Theatre,* pp.22-23.

24) 'The Work of Art', pp.239-40 and 226.

25) *Ibid.,* p.225.

26) 'What Is Epic Theatre?' first version, p.1.

27) Quoted in Nyman, *Experimental Music,* p.21.

28) Quoted in *ibid.,* p.107.

29) Quoted in Phil Slater, 'The Aesthetic Theory of the Frankfurt School'. *Cultural Studies,* VI, 196.

30)   Adorno, *Ästhetische Theorie* (Frankfurt am Main, 1970), p.292. Quoted in Slater, *loc. cit.*

31)   Adorno, 'Commitment', *New Left Review*, LXXXVII-LXXXVIII (September-December, 1974), 77.

32)   Cardew, 'A Scratch Orchestra: Draft Constitution', in *The Musical Times,* June, 1969, pp.617-18.

33)   Theatre for Pleasure or Theatre for Instruction'. *Brecht on Theatre*, p.71.

34)   'What Is Epic Theatre?' first version, pp.10 and 3.

35)   'The Modern Theatre Is Epic Theatre', *Brecht on Theatre*, p.39.

36)   'The Literarization of the Theatre', p.43.

37)   'Indirect Impact of the Epic Theatre', *Brecht on Theatre,* p.60. the original.

38)   'On the Use of Music in an Epic Theatre', *Brecht on Theatre*, p.89.

39)   'The Author as Producer', p.101.

40)   Metzger, 'Abortive Concepts in the Theory and Criticism of Music', *Die Reihe*, V (1959), 27.

41)   Quoted in Nyman, *Experimental Music*, p.1.

42)   *Ibid.*, p.91.

43)   *Ibid.*, p.123.

44)   'The Work of Art', p.230.

45)   'Theatre for Pleasure or Theatre for Instruction'. *Brecht on Theatre.* p.73.

46)   'A Short Organum for the Theatre', *Brecht on Theatre*, p.192.

47)   'Can the Present-day World Be Reproduced by Means of Theatre?' *Brecht on Theatre*, p.275.

48   'The Work of Art', p.239.

49)   Quoted in Karl Wörner, *Stockhausen: Life and Work*, trans. Bill Hopkins (London, 1973), pp.229 and 236.   5.

50)   Quoted in Nyman, *Experimental Music*, p.2.

51)   'What Is Epic Theatre?' first version, p.6.

52)   Sanguineti, 'The Sociology of the Avant-Garde', in E. and T. Burns, eds., *Sociology of Literature and Drama* (Harmondsworth, Middlesex, 1973), p.395.

53)   'The Work of Art', pp.241-43.

Chapter VII

A Revaluation of Sibelius' Symphonies

Introduction

When Sibelius began his symphonic career the symphony had been in a condition of uneven decline for seventy-five years. Whatever else it may have been, the period after the death of Beethoven was not the great age of symphonic or other sonata-type composition. These statements refer to a general trend and it is easy to think of possible exceptions: Brahms will immediately come to mind, as will Bruckner and Mahler. But even here, at those very moments that the generalization admits its exceptions, it is again confirmed in the recurrent and partially unresolved tension between form and function, or between procedures that still incline toward sonata dialectic and materials that in greater or lesser degree resist them. † What is difficult is to grasp this historical trend in its full force and import; but this we must try to do if we want to understand, roundly and specifically, the place and stature of Sibelius's achievement.

Beethoven's death in 1827 closed the great age in which, with Haydn and Mozart, he had perfected the sonata principle and changed the face of music. There is nothing mysterious about this accomplishment. The central historical point around which the age revolved was the the French Revolution; and the artistic achievements of the time belong intimately to the energies that drove towards that momentous event. This, then, is where our understanding has to begin: with the Revolution and its significance.† † Through the Revolution people both demonstrated and comprehended for the first time that history and human nature belonged to them; that it was in their power to take back these things into their own hands and to shape them for themselves. But central to this experience was the belief that the old social order needed to be overthrown because it had come to express a lie, and that it was the new order that had forged an access to the truth. This view maintained that from time to time the obvious, 'common-sense' picture of 'reality' is not true at all; it is the very denial of the truth and can be contradicted by other pictures of 'reality'. The truth now exists beyond, or behind, the present defamation of itself, and if it is to be grasped, all these stable but contradictory appearances must themselves be negated. The truth will then emerge as a new interpretation of reality, whose distinctive feature will be that it has taken up and re-embodied the original appearances in a more appropriate form: it will, in fact, be a synthesis of the earlier untruths. Now, at a certain stage this truth will also cease to be truly true; it will be contradicted and undergo the same process. Reality is thus seen as essentially contradictory, but the negation inherent in it is the principle of all life and movement. It was Hegel, born in the same year as Beethoven, who first elaborated these ideas into a total system. Reality, in this view, is dynamic: a ceaseless becoming propelled by the clash of contradictory forces. But all this

---

† Points such as these are elaborated in Chapter 1 of my book, *Twentieth-Century Symphony* (Dennis Dobson, London, 1983). As a whole, that book offers a theoretical account of the manner in which the symphony – in constantly changing musical circumstances – has developed and altered between its eighteenth-century beginnings and the present.

†† The remainder of this paragraph, and the whole of the next, recapitulates some of the argument fom the opening pages of my essay, 'Beethoven, Hegel and Marx'. While the recapitulation will be redundant for those who have read that essay, for those who have not it touches on points – about the socio-historic foundations of sonata dialectic– that are essential to my discussion of Sibelius.

unrest has a goal and finishing point. Its aim is rest, at the point where man, fully aware of these processes and his own part in them, is truly free. And this Hegel saw as the aim of the struggles of history.

It would be surprising if a relationship with reality as powerful and deeply rooted as the dialectic were not to find artistic embodiment: and indeed the sonata principle is precisely the dialectic in its musical analogue. Sonata is a way of musical thinking which generates contradictions between (say) opposing tonalities, themes, rhythmic characters, within the course of a single movement as well as over a multi-movement structure. Its starting point is the difference between the reality and the potentiality, exactly as in Hegel's dialectic. Sonata dramatizes the principle whereby something given may become something else under the driving force of contradiction: it is the highest musical articulation of the idea of forward movement through conflict. The musical style appropriate to the pre-Revolutionary conception of an unalterable human 'nature' was the Bachian principle of extension by varied, motor-like repetition. But the Revolutionary view of people as products of themselves and their own efforts in history called for nothing less than the full Beethovenian dialectic, the principle not of extension but of movement, not of repetition but of contradiction, not of variation but of thematic transformation. Where in the earlier style a piece evolves on the basis of what is already there, at the beginning, in the later it gropes ever towards a new formulation, one not given but latent within an original contradiction: it strives to become what it is *not,* on the basis of what it *is.*

Contradiction and the dialectical pursuance of it were alive in the age of the French Revolution because they were part of the consciousness and the lived experience of people who were interested in deep social – and personal – change and in the unbroken and purposeful generation of a genuinely democratic order. This state of affairs did not last. A general turning away from contradiction is apparent in all spheres of activity early in the century. Music is not exempt.

Dialectic ceases to be dialectic when it ceases to be relentless, when it loses the courage to drive itself into, through, and beyond its own contradictions. The loss of this rigour is at the heart of the symphonic problem that appeared as early as Schubert. One symptom is the replacement of *theme* by song-*tune*. Theme resists abstraction; ideally it is inseparable from its context. Tune, as self-contained, self-enclosed melody, is not only abstractable; it resists integration. The full meaning of a theme never coincides with any one of its appearances, but only with them all; each appearance is a lack and a demand, and thus an urge toward the future. The full meaning of a tune belongs to its simple presentation; further statements can vary it but not change it fundamentally and are thus in a strict sense redundant. In principle this type of melodic thinking belies contradiction: other melodies, or subjects, will be a mere arbitrary succession and a diversion, not the kind of thematic transformation that entails a generative contradiction. Further symptoms of this Romantic evasion of dialectic are the softening of the dynamic harmonic syntax of classicism, the inroads of programmaticism, and the interest in the exotic and the spectacular.

Yet while this was happening, while the content of symphonies was changing, composers clung to the old sonata forms as though these represented natural and permanent laws. The consequences were dire. Symphonic *essence* (the dialectic of contradiction) tended to become reduced to its erstwhile *appearance;* the essence was lost or at least obscured. The final purpose of symphonic practice seemed to be to fill out orthodox formal schemes – a notion that to this day riddles our textbooks. Form now stood over content, dominating it.

What was the reason for this obfuscation of the generating principle of contradiction in all forms of thought? It lies in a change in attitude to reality that can only be explained by the betrayal of the democratic ideal by the new middleclass, confirmed in the defeat of the Revolution of 1848. The change is particularly clear in European philosophy of the time. Hegel's metaphysics comes to be rejected as containing 'the principle of revolution'. Thus man's claim to alter by reason an unreasonable reality is repudiated, and in its place is recommended an assent to the existing order and the 'invariable' social laws that are supposed to control it. Comte, for instance, asks for a 'wise resignation' that will allow one 'to endure necessary evils steadfastly and without any hope of compensation'. To another philosopher the dialectic is 'treacherous', and the proper way to think about reality is to bow to the authority of inert 'facts'; truth now exists as 'a complex of ready-made objects and processes'. But by thus 'consolidating all power in the hands of those who possess this power, whoever they may be' – as Comte would have it – anti-Hegelian though soundly laid the foundations for authoritarianism. When music reflected these tendencies it did so unknowingly. The symphony tended, like those in power, to despense with true dialectic. As petrified symphonic form, Comte's 'natural, invariable laws' dominated musical content, just as they did in the authority of the state over its subjects. On another front, programmaticism in music, like the counter-revolution in philosophy, tried to bind thought to the surfaces of things.

A further consequence and cause of this artificial quiescence of reality – and a development that had a special meaning for Sibelius – was the steady growth of imperialism. Here contradiction was silenced in subtle ways. Competing international interests were temporarily subordinated to compromise settlements; or they merged in the formation of huge politico-economic alliances. In the process of shackling of the whole of society to one aim, the leadership of the economy and of the state became increasingly indistinguishable. The setting of national solidarity against class solidarity pacified internal conflicts; and the whole enterprise was sanctified under the banner of 'duty' and 'service'. Long before 1914 gave the lie to these false solutions, Nietzsche had passionately denounced the modern individual's attempt to blind himself to contradiction. The refusal to confront 'the contrariety at the centre of the universe' had, he said, created an omnipotent optimism which was 'the baneful virus of our society'. Contrariety was 'the tragedy at the heart of things'; but modern scientific man, with his 'terrestrial consonance', his 'god of engines and crucibles,' knew only 'tragic resignation' (precisely the attitude recommended by Comte!) and so was hostile to 'the truly tragic'. His comment on the effect of this on music sums up in an extreme form the trend of the entire argument. This optimism, he said, 'has succeeded with frightening rapidity in . . . . . stamping [music] with the trivial character of *divertissement . . .'*

If there was anywhere a person qualified by the circumstances of his historical predicament to restore the rigour of dialectic to the symphony, it was Sibelius. He was born in Finland in 1865, and when he began his symphonic career at the end of the century his homeland, a Grand Duchy with the Tsar as its sovereign but not a part of the Russian Empire, had just begun to suffer oppression in the form of ruthless Russification. The Finnish people were living out their own type of dialectic, meeting each assault of the Tsar with fortitude and a growing self-awareness. As early as 1892, Sibelius had joined a group of patriotic young artists who were passionately interested in the social and political function of art; there is no reason to suppose that of all his subsequent music it was only the explicitly nationalistic pieces that were true to this concern. Certainly, his Finnish audience did not suppose such a thing. But his way was not the way of programmaticism; nor could it of course be the way of Romantic flight from contradiction. Rather, it was the way of Beethoven, whom he loved above all composers.

But he faced two problems in setting out to reconnect the symphony with dialectic. The first problem was that because the nineteenth century had reduced symphonic essence to its appearance he could not take the appearance – the old form – uncritically, at face value: he would have to liberate the essence from the appearance in which it had become obscured and allow it – as content – to issue in the form adequate to it. The false status of one particular form as a 'natural, inevitable law' would be replaced by a form *expressive* of the content.

The second problem Sibelius faced was how to make the symphonic existence of contradiction plausible and intelligible. To depend upon the usual duality of thematic subjects did not really meet these criteria because it simply took contradiction for granted. He needed to find a way of bringing contradiction to consciousness – of explaining it and giving its genesis intelligible sensuous form.

How did he solve these two problems? Basically, by two means: by inventing a new technique for establishing contradiction in music; and by concentrating on the contradictory content of the symphonies and allowing that content to dictate the form, so that gradually sonata form is superseded. In Sibelius's finest music these two means unite inseparably into a single method; and this is the fusion for which he strove throughout his symphonic career.

Symphony No. 1 in E minor Op. 39

As early as the First Symphony (1898-99) Sibelius begins to work out his new technique for establishing contradiction. In the first movement, the formal first group contains a succession of ideas – really thematic fragments of irregular length – which have been strung together, some of them to form periodic wholes. Audibly, they are logically derived from the introduction; logically related to each other; and ultimately, in the process of rapid germination one by the other, *logically contradictory*. The first of them

Ex. 1

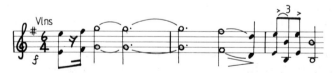

is an intense rhythmicization and simplification of a phase in the introduction – on the same notes. A suffix suggests the rhythm for the next fragment, a further concentration of the same introductory phrase, still incorporating the very same corner notes (F sharp-G-F sharp-E-B), but now with an implication of contradiction of what has gone before:

Ex. 2

This paradoxical motion – derivation and antithesis – now produces a phrase that combines the rhythm of Ex. 2 with an exaggeration and distortion of that motive's melodic characteristics; the child bears the features of the parent but utterly changes the sense:

Ex. 3

Here, in outline, is the first example of the characteristic Sibelian technique of creating contradiction. It is his principle of movement, and the essence of his symphonic thought. The classical method entrusted contradiction chiefly to objectively dualistic thematic and tonal wholes which we customarily describe as 'first' and 'second subject'; one theme manifestly contradicted another, while of course being immanently, or latently, united to it: we may call this type *manifest* contradiction. But in Sibelius's method, a motive manifestly extends another – is united to it on the surface – while being beneath the surface as it were, a contradiction of it. We may call this new type *immanent* contradiction. It was implicit in Beethoven, and indeed in the sonata idea from the beginning; what Sibelius does is to develop it radically, and to throw onto it the main burden of articulating contradiction. He intensifies the

F

technique of motivic germination to such a degree that, even more than in Beethoven, the full weight of the structure is carried by the inexhaustible power and fertility of the *cell*. Everything derives from the kinetic power contained in the smallest unit.

The full-blooded return of Ex. 1 at cue C is no formalistic reprise, but the only answer to the demand created by the rise in tension ever since its replacement by the second fragment, and then by the dynamic embodiment of the introduction's antithetical principles of rise and fall, and its semitonal motion, in the chromatic scale passages leading up to cue C. It also reveals in outline the dialectic (implicit even in the introduction) whereby this Symphony is to progress, a logic powerfully traditional despite its novel realization.

After the compelling sonata logic of the Symphony thus far, the next event is anomalous. Far from a classical symphony, where a taut yet highly supple and athletic tonal syntax enabled a modulation to a related key to be the very crisis and radical contradiction whose tension launched a new thematic group, nothing in this music's own idiom predisposes us to expect – or justifies – the arrival of a formal second subject at this point. It is not entailed by what has preceded it; it is a new beginning, and as such an interruption. Once the new section has begun, however, Sibelius immediately reconnects the music to its own life-sources. The moment of external sectional logic is forgotten: the music moves again by a powerful immanent logic. Over what is in fact a vast perfect cadence in B minor – a good example, incidentally, of Sibelius's slow-moving harmony – the first wispy, almost impressionistic fragment reveals remarkable implications. Tensions such as obtain between this fragment and the marvellously long-breathed tranquillo melody whose change of pace seems almost like a suspension of movement – tensions such as these are the contradictions by which this Symphony breathes. Equally remarkable is the breakdown of the long sinuous lines into the obsessive woodwind ostinato figure – a contradictory consequence of which we have nevertheless had forewarning, and whose bracing metrical energy we understand as being the revelation of the tensions that gave the preceding non-metrical lines their breath and flight. The astounding changes of pace in this short section anticipate some of Sibelius's later unsurpassed rhythmic feats.

The precipitate arrival of what we recognize to be the development – another formal section – stresses the point again that the Sibelian symphony is not yet in control of its own organization. Yet, once begun, it is again free to pursue its own logic: which it well does, laying bare the clean, strong lines of Sibelius's thought even when – realizing the negating powers of the chromatic principle of the introduction – it endures the most terrifying dismemberment. It is the first of Sibelius's symphonic encounters with what Nietzsche called 'the ghastly night'. We must expect recapitulation. This comes initially without awkwardness, because it is generated from within: the discovery that the rhythm and the long-held note of Ex. 3 are in common with the chromatically disintegrated second-group lines is a discovery also of the truth that wholeness is born in the midst of disintegration. For the rest, the recapitulation is skilful but the logic is different again.

Perhaps even more than the first movement, the second – like most of Sibelius's slow movements, semi-slow in the romantic tradition – simultaneously uses and denies orthodox form by making it redundant to the true, dynamic content. The Tchaikovskian opening conjures up the conventions of a static movement of romantic 'relief', but then frustrates our expectations in a way that seems calculated to disturb and unsettle. The woodwind fugato that truncates the luxuriating first section is the first episode in what is to become a rondo movement whose dynamic, developing content tends to make superfluous the formalities of its structure: it seems mainly to be written against, rather than in, rondo form. This first episode confronts the first section (thematically monolithic by comparison) with its sheer antithesis. Its momentum carries the movement along, undermining the certainties of the main theme on its next two returns, even enabling the *Rhinegold*-like broad central section to throw up some of the fleetest, most ephemeral shapes in the movement; but its implications are most truly realized in the final episode, in which an organic doubling of pace quite leaves behind the slow movement and its conventions. As in the first movement, the moment of most horrifying dissolution reveals – or rather, creates – the centre that can withstand such destruction: the shape of the fury at its height discloses the outline of the first theme. The recovery thus far is immanent, logical and necessary; the form of the immediate reappearance of the theme, merely sewn on and oblivious of what has intervened, is not.

The principle of cellular germination leads the brilliant, hard-edged scherzo ever further away from its starting point; but the discoveries of the previous movements are germane to this, and in the outward journey the centre is repeatedly glimpsed – each time anew as it is ever subsumed into the perspective of a wider orbit. The difference is that this move-ment is a game: rough, elegant, precise, dramatic, playing at life's tragedies without becoming them, spurred on by its own inexhaustible – indeed Beethovenian – energy. The involve-ment of the other movements in this is sometimes almost literal. For instance, the darting woodwind figure beginning in the fifth bar after cue A has been transplanted from the link to the first movement's development:

Ex. 4

(i) First Movement

(ii) Third Movement

and the line on the violins that becomes prominent in the vicinity of cue C is an elaboration of bars 9 to 14 of the introduction. Where growth by motivic proliferation is so fertile, the *lento* trio is out of place. But in the very act of accepting the trio convention and the Romantic tendency to regard that section as a retreat, Sibelius turns it to critical dramatic effect: in accepting it he destroys it. True symphonist and realist, he cannot for long accept the escape: the external world forces itself three times upon his consciousness through the haze and destroys the Elysium of sweet sounds and aromas. Reality intrudes by way of prominent first-movement figures, particularly one from the second group; the final harp glissando is the vanishing of a dream, clearing the way for the return to more urgent business. For play can be serious too; and in scherzo and trio Sibelius contrasts two types of pleasurable activity and shows the one to be mere impotent flight, the other to be engaged, concerned with a problematic reality at its heart, though in the form of play.

The recall of part of the introduction to the first movement at the start of the finale is not only a step in the direction of integration – to become so characteristic of Sibelius – but a comprehension, for which we have had to wait three movements, of the seminal and germinating power of the introduction. Its function as a generative source, as the basic urge out of which the Symphony grows, is at last understood: explicit use is made of the fertility of the introduction, as no fewer than ten distinct germs are spawned before the end of the first group – to say nothing of their variants – which now derives from the introduction also by way of a change of pace. Generally, this is the weakest movement – because the most derivative, the least authentic. The development is strong, because self-generative like the opening. So too is the start of the recapitulation: here is a wonderful emergence, what the development has yielded through turmoil. But the sprawling second subject owes its existence to external decree; obscuring contradiction under its false semblance, it no longer expresses duality but seduces attention away from it. It well illustrates how inapposite form may prevent contradiction from fully appearing. In recapitulation its attempted apotheosis is bombast.

Significantly, the Symphony reaches its true goal afterwards, outside any pre-given structure. In the seven bars after cue X the original, predominantly downward, tendency of the introduction is reversed in a passage of upward chromatic movement that nevertheless comprehends its opposite; it is one of the best moments in the Symphony, anticipating the ecstatic suffering of later Sibelius and marred only by a single unctuous cliché, making the point that even here Sibelius is not yet fully himself.

Symphony No. 2 in D Op. 43

The weight of an inherited formal apparatus lies somewhat less heavily on the Second Symphony (1901) than on the First. Where the effort of the earlier work was in denying the conventions, the effort of this Symphony is spent rather in pointing the way beyond them. This is in some measure its strength; its weakness is that most of the effort in this regard is spent closest to the beginning, so that in general each succeeding movement is less radical in its handling of the problem than the previous one – a fact that is inseparable from the greater quality of each movement compared to its successor. A further trait that distinguishes this work from the First Symphony – and which was increasingly to preoccupy Sibelius as part of his search for adequate form – is the way each movement picks up, in mood at least, where the last left off. The wish to make each movement a logical emergence is of course most evident in the way the finale is conceived in the womb of the scherzo, which subsequently gives birth to it(this has an obvious precedent in Beethoven's Fifth). There have been many attempts in history to tighten and integrate the symphonic span; but the tendency characteristic of Sibelius, to subsume the multi-movement symphony into a single, patently evolving structure, in which each movement in some sense continues the previous one rather like the succession of acts in a drama, is not typical of either the classical or the Romantic symphony.

The fine, lithe opening movement is the most authentic and accomplished in the first two symphonies. Here, for the purpose of freeing itself, sonata essence is in the process of corroding the old sonata form. Like so much in Sibelius, the movement confounds commentators who bring their old categories to it. A symptom of such confusion is the tired argument about where the 'second group' begins – or even what it is. Some, basing their argument on the altered key in the recapitulation, will say that the 'second group' begins at the *poco allegro* (at cue C). But what is the meaning of the concept when the new melodic idea shares the same pulsating, repeated-note accompanimental figure that had characterized so much of the first-group accompaniment, and had opened the Symphony; when it seems on that account to belong to the 'first group'; and when it is just one of the many melodic ideas that have proliferated, in typical Sibelian fashion, since the beginning of the movement? The confusion remains only so long as we assume that forms are always true to the content they are meant to express: only so long as we confer upon forms a universal validity. In understanding Sibelius we have to understand that forms are only historically, temporarily, valid.

The dramatic-ironic force of this movement depends to some extent on our believing that nothing could disturb the carefree pastoral mood of the chirping woodwind theme of the opening. Though we know that it is finite – it is built very evidently upon a series of phrases that rise and fall, grow out of silence and return into it, like respiration – its very ability to go round and round repetitively seems to belie its finitude. But it really is finite; and the implications of finitude are that it does not comprise the whole. This is the meaning of the cadence ('interrupted', both technically and literally) and hiatus eight bars after cue A, and of what immediately follows: the forlorn phrase for flutes, with its minor-key inflexion, and the upward-swinging phrase it generates, with its dark bassoon colouring, rhythmic asymmetry and tense supporting drum-roll. These are aspects of the insecurity that has suddenly replaced the pristine stability of the opening:

Ex. 5

Confronted with their own contradiction, the original certainties have simply been destroyed, posing a problem for the Symphony, the solution of which must depend at the very least on the discovery of a mode that can comprehend both these experiences. Symphony is the logic of contradictions; and the long unison violin theme that is potentialized in the heart of the menacing, trilling culmination of these disturbing bars is already a brave retort:

Ex. 6

Other responses to the conflict are a rich string figure, Tchaikowsky-like in the nature of its grief; and a more optimistic – though still sombre-hued – wind passage. (The antiphony of the instrumental blocks is characteristic of Sibelius.) But it is not until the assertive F sharp minor passage after cue C – for some the 'second group', as we have seen – that momentum and confident thematicism are restored, forty-one bars after the relatively minor first crisis. The reappearance of

the ostinato accompaniment, moreover, for the first time since
the crisis, reinforces this feeling of restoration. Partial the
recovery may be: the initial D major has after all been lost, and
it will be some time before it is found again. But where the
opening pastoral theme ever subsided passively into stillness,
this passage is wave upon wave of surging crescendo; and the
jagged, tritonal incisions by the woodwind against the diatonic
flow bear witness to at least an attempt now to admit the reality
of dualism.

Though the arrival of what we recognize as development is
in one sense a logical consequence of contradiction, in another
it still declares subservience to *a priori* schema: it begins as a
new section after an orthodox close of great finality, even in the
dominant. The destructive pole of the dualism reigns through
most of this development, the tritone driving the music
through the abyss to the point of virtual extinction, melodyless
and barely audible on a G sharp kettledrum pedal, an annihilating tritone from the home key. Yet the paradox is that
hope is fertilized in negation: the pedal G sharps call up the
fount and starting point of the music (the repeated-note string
figure) and the opening theme, unheard since the thirtieth bar.
And the striving Ex. 7 (ii) that brings back the generic 'second
subject' – a substantial recovery – is made with and from the
very fragments of nothingness, Ex. 7 (i), from the earlier part of
the development:

Ex. 7

Yet more remarkable, the tritone itself is turned to heroic
purpose as the urgent striving phrase, Ex. 7 (ii), mounts ever

higher in a polyphony in which the beginning of each phrase is a whole tone above the previous one, thus incarnating the tritone in a whole-tone scale over nine steps.

What happens after this point is recapitulatory rather than 'the recapitulation': external schema has been subsumed into a pure organic re-creation and regeneration of earlier material, necessary only because the music is winning back wholeness and identity from fragmentation and non-identity. And it is a continuing process: D, for example, is suddenly present, but only as a pedal, and it will be lost again before D becomes present as a tonic, some twenty-odd bars later. Then we shall understand what this music has wrought from its experience of dismemberment, as the formerly disparate and contradictory ideas of the exposition are taken up in a passage which synthesizes them into a whole of expansive calm and assurance, and finally ecstatic declamation. Here too the shape of some of the ideas has been forged precisely from the disfigured form in which they appeared in the development. This whole passage up to the tempo change before cue O might be studied closely as the first in which Sibelius's greatness as a symphonic thinker becomes truly manifest. After this, the ensuing reprise can only seem unfortunate. The logic by which the music of the exposition is played again is that of an external authority from whose shackles Sibelius was still struggling to become free. Unlike the foregoing passage, its logic and truth are not wholly of its own making, skilful and telling though its variations upon the exposition may be.

In the slow movement there is also an evident attempt to supersede inherited form: most importantly, by combining it with a highly dramatic use of the technique of immanent contradiction. We saw similar combinations in the First Symphony – but none quite like this – in which the dramatic, accomplished and sustained use of the technique gives to the movement the appearance of a sonata form whose development has been woven into – or rather into and after – the exposition of each of its subjects. The first subject section especially moves qualitatively far enough away from its origins and over sufficient length to be different from a normal sonata structure, or for that matter a binary movement. The contradictions generated by each subject-section are dramatic moments, akin in that way too to sonata development; but a problem here is that Sibelius cannot repeat his exposition without also repeating its 'developmental' consequences, since he is committed to sectional repitition, however varied. Therefore what was once dramatic is not so twice – a difficulty only partly solved by the expansion and further development to which the sections are subjected during their reprise. This problem of dramatic development being repeated was not one that was encountered by the classical symphony which, once its development had become the dramatic centre and thus an 'autonomous' section within a ternary form, in place of its being part of a binary form both of whose sections were repeatable, did not play its development again.

The movement takes up the concerns of the first. The opening section attempts to defy finitude by combining it (in the form of the theme introduced by the bassoons) with the seemingly infinite continuousness of the undulating pizzicato line; besides, the finite theme itself, though it clearly rises out of silence and dies away into it, aspires through its modality and the character of its inflexions to a chant-like condition of endlessness. But it soon runs dry, and encounters its own end in a final phrase which it repeats four times. Now the theme is able to go on only in a perverted form; it strives to continue; a new string variant – already a little agitated – implies the subsequent thorough disruption; and the import of the conflict that follows is that if the theme is to continue it must relinquish its former state. To go on it must accept its own disintegration, its dissolution into another mode – a reality which it at first resists – and enter the truth that real continuity means death as much as it means life: that it is death which activates the principles of continuity in life. Against the attacks of its own decaying form, the theme struggles to hold on to an earlier shape (x in Ex. 8) while the destructive process revitalizes the tritone, turning its whole-tone scale embodiment – used by the first movement at its herioc height – to disruptive effect:

Ex. 8

The fact that the second subject:

Ex. 9

owes its existence to the decaying form of the first (*y* in Ex. 8)
does not make this new theme as internally logical as one might
wish. Sibelius's thematic germination is to become, and has
already been, better than this, because controlled by a more
immanent necessity. Rather like the corresponding stage in the
opening movement of the First Symphony, this is almost a new
beginning. The answer this section seeks to the problem of
thematic finitude is the spawning of new shapes; and this only
drives the music quickly into contradictions, and a crisis
beyond which a heavy version of a motive from the subject is
unable to progress. The dramatic impasse gives Sibelius the
opportunity he wants to bring round his first-subject section
again. Indeed, the movement exploits impasse: it cannot find,
nor even adumbrate, a state which is beyond the disintegration
with which it wrestles, and yet can encompass it. In its way,

that was the achievement of the first movement. Apparently it is of no avail here.

With its hellish flickering lights and Mephistophelean virtuosity, the scherzo is a symbolic embodiment of the disruptive, negating force at the heart of this Symphony. The movement offers a clear late-stage articulation, in all its fierce fiendish glory, of what the previous movements encountered as their internalized Other, as their immanent Negation. Here that diabolical force is openly declared in its own terms, not merely experienced passively in terms of its effects. And one might say that it is externalized now because it is at last fully understood; no longer is it only an unintelligible 'symptom'. If the constituents of a contradiction are not manifest, this, then, is the way Sibelius will lay them bare. The movement is a crucial stage in the drive towards the truth: here the 'hidden' component of an antagonism has finally, by means of the Symphony's sustained effort, been brought to the surface. This is the first instance in the Sibelius symphonies of a procedure which the composer was to make persistent use of, and greatly to refine.

Until the remarkable happening in the second appearance of the trio, this is a formal movement: the static co-presence of scherzo and trio depends upon a set of assumptions that are patently not those most representative of the Symphony so far. Yet the intrusion of the scherzo after the trio, though a formal reprise, is at first dramatic: the limpid and beautiful trio had seemed so fragile, so vulnerable, in this company – an impression confirmed when the scherzo violently bursts in upon it in a confrontation that dramatically sums up the central issue of the Symphony. We know the trio is vulnerable because of the experiences of the first two movements, and because thematically and by way of a general mood it is related to the pastoral opening theme of the Symphony, and to the second subject of the slow movement. Like its first-movement relative, the trio theme has a tendency to go round and round. It seems that it must inevitably be overwhelmed here by that of which its circularity causes it to seem oblivious, as happened in the first movement and indeed in the scherzo the first time. But now the simple, folk-like trio melody finds the resources of expansion and growth adequate to its task; by true Sibelian cellular germination it gives birth to the majesty of the finale theme, in whose sunlight the hell-fire light of the scherzo is powerless to prevail.

It is significant in terms of Sibelius's musico-historical enterprise that this finale – symbol of the Symphony's achievement in the Beethovenian sense – should not be merely posited but that it should emerge triumphantly, and without a break, from the very tissue of the previous movement. In so doing, it demonstrates persuasively that its logic is its own. But ironically – and this is symptomatic of a now familiar problem – the movement is also the sheerest submission to bad conventions. Its material is static and intractable (especially the over-long second subject, with its folk-like individuality and Tchaikowsky-like pathos), its development an academic procedure, its repetitions gratuitous, its peroration bombastic in the way of so many nineteenth-century symphonic finales. Written to formula, it is unequal to the task of satisfactorily resolving contradictions of the subtlety and complexity of the rest of the Symphony, especially of the first movement. For instance, it ignores rather than comprehends the meaning of the scherzo, banishing it instead of making it part of its very own principle; the reappearance of fragmentation in the development is a mere formality. Except for some simple thematic relationships, the triumph of this movement is not wrought in the terms given by the problems of the previous movements; it is arguable that it does not even 'belong' to the rest of the Symphony.

Symphony No. 3 in C Op. 52

Sibelius's Third Symphony (1904-07) is in a sense a reaction to the excesses of the first two. Intent on making ever more translucent the process of symphonic thought, the composer now turned deliberately to classical models. Here he could discover at its life-source the essence of symphony.

The first movement is in many ways the most classical of all Sibelius's symphonic movements. It is not typical of his symphonic method to pose at the very outset a manifest opposition between full, objective subject-groups. The second group contradicts the C major of the first by being in B minor; its return in the recapitulation in E minor – the key of the mediant minor rather than that of the leading note – follows in spirit the classical precedent by being less remote from the home tonic. But there are also important departures from classical practice. We hear the principal member of the second group as the full exposition of an idea that was already present within the first: its most characteristic cell is audible in the oboes, clarinets and horns from the fifth bar after cue 2, an immanent duality whose genealogy can be traced back further even than the foregoing chromatic tensions, to (say) the early F sharp-C tritone in the strings before cue 1. This fact is given telling emphasis in the way the second group is introduced dramatically by a strident F sharp sounding (as dominant to the new tonic, B) against the hitherto almost unbroken tonic pedal C.

It is this logic – which shows the second-subject group to exist immanently, but unambiguously, prior to its 'formal' presentation – that makes its subsequent structural appearance inevitable rather than schematic. Such clear logical generation of a second group, so that it comes as the externalization of what was formerly internal, was not the typical classical method; this exposition is remarkable for its fusion of Sibelius's technique of immanent contradiction with the classical one of manifest contradiction. Sibelius's characteristic method is to show us the 'how' of contradiction; the characteristic classical way was to reveal, as a *fait accompli*, the 'what'. Here Sibelius combines: he shows 'how' the 'what' comes into being. Only the speed, the motivic flexibility, the taut and cogent logic of the movement could have made such a fusion – and particularly such a recovery of classical method and form – possible. An important aspect of these qualities is something we may describe as the music's objectivity. Its freedom from the kind of subjectivity we associate with a

Romantic self-absorption means that it cannot be indulged but must only be developed. Indeed, there is little enough in it to indulge: classically the music sets out from the simplest, bare bones, which refer us ever into their future for the elaboration of their meaning.

Yet it is clear that this is not a repeatable solution, or Sibelius's final solution, to the problem of form. He resurrects classical form but only at the expense of some of his own most significant content: the movement, for all its precision, its perfect matching of ideas to their embodiment and development, has not the profundity, the peculiar and appropriate significance, of the first movements of the two previous symphonies. Sibelius can bring to life the classical world but only at the price of the deepest relevancy to his own. Lacking an idiom naturally suited to classical formulation, a classical idiom whose life is inseparable from its classical form, his only solution is to inhibit the expressive powers of his own idiom. Where the classical masters spoke naturally in sentences that, however brief, were capable of bearing a profound meaning, Sibelius, trying to be equally brief, is only sententious, and sometimes skittish. His is by nature a different idiom; his profundity does not live in classical structures. Though doubtless this frontal encounter with classicism was necessary to his development, it tends to lead here to an artificial restraint. When he comes to write his slow movement, the need to find one that is in keeping with the *allegro moderato* means that the powerful expressive world of the slow movement of the Second Symphony is closed to him. If he now produces one of his slightest movements – though nevertheless one with secret depths that are easily turned into shallows by too rapid performance – this is a measure of the inhibition imposed on him by his general formal and stylistic orientation. Even so, the movement is less a classical piece than a Romantic intermezzo-type slow movement that has been thinned out and scaled down to size. Simpler even than a series of variations, it is in a somewhat free strophic form.

But in the finale Sibelius surpasses these limitations. He uses the classical experience not in such a way that it inhibits his musical sensibility, but so that it directs it. The classical symphony, in order to be made relevant to his own world, had to be radically reinterpreted. This is the guiding principle he had already been seeking somewhat haphazardly in the first two symphonies, and whose greatest embodiment he found in the late music of Beethoven. And it is in the finale of the Third Symphony that Sibelius for the first time gives life to this principle with total assurance. Here, more thoroughly than anywhere previously in his symphonies, the technique of immanent contradiction is the true dialectical propeller of the movement. Notice the speed with which ideas proliferate and create an order in which the numerous melodic entities are as logically related and interdependent as they are logically contradictory – the explanation of the change of tempo every few bars. Yet close observation reveals that the old classical structure has been subsumed into the movement, for all its apparent flouting of tradition, and that it now informs the movement from within. If this form lives here at all, it does so not as formula or pattern but as the consequence of a certain way of thinking. The peculiarity of its life is the truth of tradition when that tradition is still alive and growing. By the same principle this third movement is not only finale but scherzo as well; it combines the tradition of the light, rapid, dancing motion of scherzo with that of the perorative finale.

In order to grasp the way the past has been captured and still lives as present in this movement, we must try to unravel the elements that have been synthesized in the new whole. We can perhaps recognize a 'first group' in C major, up to cue 2, and a 'second group' in the relative minor thereafter; a short transition leading to a varied counter-exposition, with the second group now in the subdominant minor; and a subsequent development. The new (*con energia*) section that replaces recapitulation is, in this view, the real finale: what has gone before is scherzo. The fusion is an intensification of the linking of the corresponding movements in the previous Symphony. But comparison of the 'subject-groups' shows that this is really not a sonata structure – not even the 'scherzo' part of it: the flute motive nine bars after cue 2 is theoretically the first melodic fragment of the 'second group', but it springs directly from the previous motives, and is no more different from any of them than most of them are from each other.

The fusion of scherzo and finale is only the most obvious instance in this Symphony of Sibelius's preoccupation with making the diverse symphonic frame what it once was: a taut, integrated structure capable of registering the implications of dialectical thought over a large span. Equally important, and of prime significance for the understanding of the long-range symphonic purpose of this work, is the way in which the 'finale' – the triumphant culmination of the third movement – is the fulfilment of an aspiration latent even within the main subjects of the first movement The climactic hymnic marching-song marks the arrival of a new order, embryonically present in the sudden and frequent chorale-like strivings of the foregoing movements. One such moment is the coda to the first movement. This coda realizes more fully an urge expressed at the end of the exposition, and it is prepared for by a dry, athematic and asymmetrical pizzicato passage that in its disruption of the preceding melodic flow powerfully suggests the dissolution of the old order as a condition for the appearance of the new. When it arrives, the new, however different from the old, is yet felt to issue from it; and analysis reveals why. The main subjects of the first movement had shared a common basic shape, Ex. 10 (i), heard at its clearest first in the opening bars of the Symphony (ii) and later in a modification (cue 13) of the principal member of the second-subject group (iii):

Ex. 10

The coda now emphasizes and extends the descent through a fourth:

Ex. 11

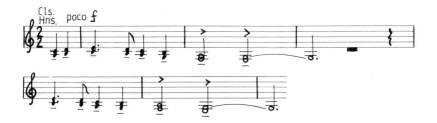

The second movement intermittently erupts into its own chorale-like variation of the basic shape, in a form suggested by Ex. 11, for instance soon after cue 6:

Ex. 12

The fullest articulation of the 'chorale' urge occurs, as in the preceding movement, at its end. The first two movements at times suggest disintegration; the third movement pursues that disintegration to finality, in the form of a development which splits what are in any case only fragments to atoms, and whirls them about. The marching-hymn to which it ultimately gives birth could not have emerged a moment earlier; anticipated three times in this movement, each more fully than the last, it comes to establish the dispensation so long awaited: it is the thematic fulfilment of the Symphony, an elaboration of the basic shape, which it still includes in its full, original outline (*x*):

Ex. 13

The Second Symphony had shown a tendency of each later movement to emerge dramatically from its predecessor, and of the multi-movement symphony thus to appear as a logically evolving structure. In the Third we find Sibelius similarly concerned to make the sequence of movements seem rational rather than merely conventional. He achieves this particularly through the special use of the chorale-like passages. The fact that the first two movements end after substantial expressions of the 'chorale' element, suggests that this immanent urge, striving for fulfilment, has brought each movement to the point where it is logically superseded: in the face of what is both an aspiration and a demand, each movement can only end, and give way to another.

Symphony No. 4 in A minor Op. 63

The Fourth (1910-11) is Sibelius's first great symphonic master-piece. In it we can witness a resolution of the problems which had beset him, and to which he had been seeking answers, in the first three symphonies. It is perhaps no paradox that a work which represents the first moment of resolution and synthesis in Sibelius's symphonic style is also one that wrestles with the most profound dualities. The seriousness and gravity of the work's concern, its intensity of concentration, is precisely what explains this first great moment of maturation in Sibelius's symphonic style. But the Fourth is not to be judged only in the context of Sibelius's symphonies. When all else is said and done, it will still demand to be taken for what it is: one of the supreme tragic statements of Western music.

The central symbol in it is the tritone, the interval most destructive of tonal sense; its peculiar negating force has caused it to be known since the Middle Ages as *diabolus in musica*. While this work was being written, Sibelius feared for both the country he loved and the art to which he was dedicated. His precise attitude at this time to contemporary music is not easy to define; but among the comments he made about it during his life are that the 'themes often seemed artificial, the elaboration mechanical', that the instrumentation was frequently 'too showy', that too much contemporary music had 'very little connection with life'. At any rate, he let it be known that his new Symphony might be regarded as 'a protest against the compositions of today'. There was nothing, he said, *'absolutely nothing of the circus about it'*. On the political front, Finnish autonomy was again being assaulted by Russian imperialism, in 1910 more seriously than ever before. Sibelius hated 'all empty talk on political questions, all amateurish politicising'. 'I have tried', he said, 'to make my contribution in another way'. This distinction and this commitment stand out in a comment he made in August 1910, in a letter that illuminates the deep relationship between the Fourth Symphony and the circumstances in Finland at the time. 'Politics,' he wrote, 'do not interest me at present. For I cannot help in any other way than by labouring "for king and country". I am working on my new symphony'.

The tritone is present as early as the first bar of the Symphony, both horizontally and vertically, between the C which by its firm unisonal entrance initially proposes itself as tonic, and the F sharp that quickly undermines it (the true tonic soon emerges as A minor):

Ex. 14

If we want to think that a residue of the old, slow introduction lingers in the opening bars we need not be wrong. But so little will Sibelius be concerned here to preserve the superficial appearances of sonata form that we ought not to be surprised when the *quasi adagio* tempo does not give way to any classical allegro. The most pervasive tritonal relation in the first twenty-odd bars is that expressed vertically between these same notes, C and F sharp. An event of crucial importance takes place at the end of this passage. During a steady crescendo over three bars, the C-F sharp tritone is asserted melodically and then emphatically resolved in favour of G, three times (violins, cellos, horns) and fortissimo – the first time since the opening bar that this dynamic level has been reached. It is a magnificent surge of optimism, owing everything to the possibility which is now discovered in the tritone as an interval whose annihilating tensions can also be deployed creatively: by directing its energies onto the G, the interval establishes a context for itself, and so incarnates a meaning. Here, for the first time in the Symphony, the tritone has been redeemed:

Ex. 15

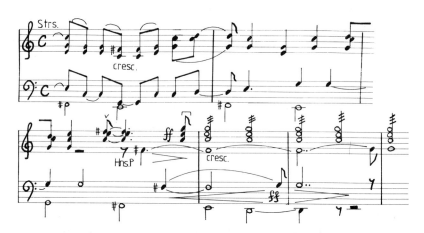

The passage is clearly scored; how often its point is obscured by unintelligent performance! The dialectic of these bars con-

tinues to unfold by bold convolutions, as almost immediately a
bare, heavy C sharp tritonally contradicts the G, destroying the
achievement it stands for. A bar later the original F sharp
reappears in the bass to provide a resolute answer to that C
sharp: since F sharp makes a perfect fifth with C sharp, the
latter is denied its negating power, and is instead made to
confirm the incipient modulation to F sharp major. To put this
another way: the note, C sharp, that from the standpoint of G is
negation, becomes affirmation from the standpoint of F sharp,
helping to liberate F sharp to the status of tonic to which it has
aspired from the beginning.

Second-subject hunters among commentators often speak of
the passage immediately after the modulation to F sharp major
as the orthodox new subject. This tonal shift is certainly a
moment of tension, but it is only one such moment among
many and it has no right to the kind of prominence conferred
by orthodox analytical categories. The string motive (beginning A, B, D sharp, C sharp) is a transposed variant of the
opening bar, with the force of an exclamation; at best one can
say that the old second subject has been subsumed, or sub-
limated, into this passage. Sibelius had before this Symphony
written nothing more beautiful than the music of deep,
measured lyricism and calm that ensues. A warm light suddenly transfigures the world – not because the tritone has ceased to
exist, but because it is redeemed by a context that wrings a very
human expressiveness from it:

Ex. 16

The replacement of E sharp by E natural at cue E is the
beginning of an attempt to seek regions closer to A. But all that
the dominant of A is able to see is A sharp, given out at once by
the double-basses. It is a tritonal relation that plunges the lower

strings deep into the depths of their registers. The tritone, it
now seems, is the condition of all movement. No step can be
taken without encountering it; the negative lies at the heart of
being. The fine stark string lines, bereft of all solidarity, of
familiar harmonic and tonal supports, soon disintegrate
further into an endlessly roving tremolo figuration founded
upon two whole-tone scales a semitone apart: phraseless,
arhythmic, amelodic, without tonality or functional harmonic
movement, the music becomes a void that whirls mindlessly
about itself. Yet what is most remarkable of all is that in the end
so much violent emptiness can have a purpose. The long-held
wind notes that explode at length into a tritone appear at
measured intervals, each step occurring a semitone higher than
the last. When the long note becomes A, the orchestra braces
itself in anticipation – then throws A forcefully into the bass,
and soon establishes it as the tonic. The strength that brings a
structure and an organisation to this experience of despair is
precisely the meaning that is wrought from it. Now the world is
radiant again as the warm lyrical music returns, a vision
realized in the home-key of A: it is much more and much less
than recapitulation. But, finally, the beauty is not enough. At
its end the movement suddenly remembers its beginning. This
retrospective glance to the first bar pinpoints once more the
tritone as the central and still unresolved problem. It is a dying
fall of icy foreboding.

As in the two preceding symphonies, Sibelius here wants the
succession of movements to appear rational. Thus, remember-
ing the achievement of the first, the scherzo begins with a sense
of wholeness and stability, deploying lines in which the tritone
takes its place with affability; and while its tonality is F major –
a key quite new to the Symphony – it starts melodically with the
same sustained A on which the first movement had ended. The
fusion, across the space that divides the movements, is uncanny. The approach to the tritone is playful: up to cue B the
scherzo enjoys light skirmishes with it, a kind of teasing
flirtation that nevertheless gives it an embodiment and a
limited sense. Evidently this is unsatisfactory. At cue B the
abrupt displacement of the graceful triple by a rigid duple

rhythm, and the bare octave lines, herald the appearance of the tritone in its destructive aspect. Soon the tritone is totally disembodied, floating in empty space. With no better solution to offer, the first section steals back up, curls itself around the interval and tries again. If the *tranquillo* flute passages do not charm the tritone into compliance nothing will. But more than charm is needed to deal with this Mephistophelean force, which at cue **K** begins to show its full implications. What was formerly implicit:

Ex. 17

is now fully revealed:

Ex. 18

As the negative that has been ignored, the new section— apparently the generic trio – comes to shame the frivolity, the undeveloping repetitiveness, of the main body of the scherzo. It hurls us back into the night of the first-movement development, but with this difference: that while the darkness there was suffered to some purpose, here it has all the force of a horrible surprise. In the complacency of a partial solution such nothingness had not been reckoned with. F, the home tonic, represented until the end as an internal pedal, and B, its tritonal antithesis, which makes strong claim to being the new tonal centre – these two lock in a fruitless, annihilating strife. At the end all that is left of the original positives is the merest ghost of the first theme, which flickers to life within the alien domain of B and is promptly smothered, and a vague memory of the principal tonic, struck lifelessly upon timpani soli. These are also all that remain of the spirit of reprise that in a classical work would have brought back the first part of the scherzo at this point. Here no return is possible because no pre-established order has meaning in the face of such internal contradictions. Perhaps more than any other piece of music, this movement makes it clear why recapitulation has today become problematic. Equally important, it is the final vindication of the necessity of Sibelius's search for appropriate form.

The principal tonic of the scherzo, F, had been maintained as a single unbroken thread on the second violins throughout the holocaust of the last part of the movement. This, and the fact that at least a shadow of the original thematic identity twitched with life at the end, is the fortitude that enables the Symphony to progress beyond this point, the nearest music has ever come to self-extinction in mid-flight. The slow movement begins in the only way that, rationally, it can: with the fragments, the disorientation, the barrenness, bequeathed to it by the scherzo. Yet the search for a new key (none is established at the beginning) is a search for a new orientation towards the experience, evidently satisfied only by the discovery of a tonality (C sharp minor) as far on the dominant side of the main key of the Symphony (A minor) as that of the scherzo (F major) was on the subdominant. The first two bars, indeed, remember A minor in an imprecise allusion to its tonic and dominant. As might be expected, the music is riddled with the tritone, which lives in it both melodically and harmonically. Yet in its very disjointedness the music reveals a contour to which one can ascribe a meaning and a hope. It is only the outline of an aspiration, the germ of what is to become a passionate imprecation, but it is forged from the very stuff of despair, by way, for instance, of the initial flute phrases rising through fifths:

Ex. 19

and the superimposed fifths of the clarinet's comment:

Ex. 20

which are already the cells around which the horns are to fashion their optimism:

Ex. 21

The logical extrapolation of motives gives rise not to an endless chain of monistically related entities, but to oppositions within a broadly monothematic context. The broken fragments are – and remain – tonally restless; it is only through the horn motive and its later variants that the music achieves a secure tonal footing. The movement follows the pattern of an extended alternation between the shattered relics of its own history, and the hope that arises from the ruins. This gives the movement its form, one not describable in straightforward traditional terms. The big theme grows passionately in opposition to (yet out of)

the non-being around it; it strives to banish the notion of the
tritone and declaim only a stirring diatonic melody that
embraces pure fifths and fourths. Sufficient though this may be
for recovery, it cannot ultimately be the answer to the
Symphony's great central concern: at the end, even after the
final lyrical exclamation, the emptiness remains. The tritone
still inhabits it. It is still inhuman, alien. Though the music
has come a long way since the end of the first movement, the
tritone still sounds almost exactly as it did then.

Each movement has tried to solve the problem of the tritone
and each in its own way has succeeded and failed. The concrete
particulars of this complex of failure and success constitute the
accumulated experience out of which the finale is able to drive
the problem toward a true solution. Here, as elsewhere in the
Symphony, there is no doubt about the intimate connection
between the new movement and its predecessor, for the A major
of its beginning leans strongly towards C sharp minor and
deploys a theme that was anticipated on clarinets and bassoons
in the fourteenth bar before the end of the slow movement. If
the finale begins buoyantly, capable soon of summoning bells,
it is because the music has learnt how to be gay in the face of
contradiction. But it is a tragic gaiety, very different from either
the frivolity of the scherzo or the passing rapture of the first
movement. Where the first movement discovered nothingness
and contradiction at the heart of being, the finale has won
through to a creative involvement with these things. Duality is
the essence of its dynamic. What strikes one immediately about
the finale is the sheer quantity of widely diversified material it
contains. Outspoken antitheses pursue and give life to one
another, establishing at the same time a harmonious large-
scale organization and a stable structure. The tritone is now not
a threat to the music but the source of its vigour:

Ex. 22

and the root of the principle of contradiction by which it lives and expands. A major and E flat major meet over a substantial length twice in this movement; but far from being a collision between opposed energies, this meeting of antitheses provides the music with two symmetrically placed arches capable of gathering antagonisms to an apex and transcending them by releasing their structural potential.

The long coda-like conclusion is the moment of the Symphony's return to, and at the same time final victory over, chaos. It is this fusion that gives these pages, among the most profound in all music, their power to move us so deeply. In the fragmentation, in the pervasive grind of the tritone and its associated chromaticism, we recognize the chaos; but in the passion that welds the blasted pieces into a new whole of anguished beauty, we comprehend the triumph. It is an experience of chaos unlike any other in the Symphony, for it is a chaos redeemed by being humanized; from it has been wrenched a meaning and a value. This conclusion reveals the tragedy that underlies the gaiety. The finale can be gay *because* of the tragedy: for it is in the enduring of this chaos that man's potential discovers itself. 'I begin, like Beethoven', said Sibelius, writing about the Fourth Symphony the year after its completion, 'to believe that strength is really human morality. I mean, of course, strength in its highest and widest sense.'

Symphony No. 5 in E Flat Op. 82

The Fourth and Fifth Symphonies seem at first sight to belong to quite unrelated worlds. The Fourth is a work of tragedy, of horror, of darkness; the Fifth is a work of light, life and a boundless, expansive energy. But in the difference is the connection: one may say the world of the Fifth Symphony has been won for it by the suffering of the Fourth. A unity between the two pieces is suggested also by the remarks Sibelius made around the time of their composition. During our discussion of the Fourth Symphony we found that the following remark by Sibelius bore a significant relationship to the work: '. . .

strength is really human morality . . .'; and a pupil of Sibelius's reported that in the autumn of 1914 – that is, at the time of the conception of the Fifth Symphony – the composer began to think deeply about civilization, admiring what he took to be its 'moral strength and courage', its capacity to endure great hardship. The tragic ethic of heroic suffering was a theme that preoccupied Sibelius throughout the creative part of his life, but perhaps at no time more profoundly than during the period which gave birth to the Fourth and Fifth Symphonies.

A minor is the key of the Fourth; the new Symphony takes its point of inception as E flat major, a key – perhaps significantly – a tritone from the former. These two keys are the central supports of the finale of the Fourth; and while that movement wrenches a tragic gaiety from its experience of the 'the contrariety at the centre of the universe', the first movement of the Fifth celebrates the energy that can draw its life from suffering. But this great movement poses a problem for the rest of the Symphony. It is so triumphantly conclusive in what we shall recognize as its festive demonstration of the dialectic of change that in the next two movements – since the composer was committed to having them – his only options were to repeat himself or to simplify his vision. Here perhaps we are close to the reason why the Fifth Symphony gave Sibelius more trouble than any other.

At the first performance in 1915 the work existed in four separate movements. Sibelius must have felt that the piece had an unsatisfactory form, a form not truly expressive of its content, for he withdrew it and when the second version appeared the following year the first two movements had been synthesized. Even so, it was revised again; the final version dates from 1919. But by realizing the essence of the Symphony so brilliantly in the great compound first movement, this recomposition perhaps emphasized still more the inadequacy of the rest of the work. To put the point a little too sharply, one might say that the Fifth is a Symphony in one movement but with two postludes. This view isolates both its strength and its weakness. It is a great but flawed work, its weakness being that it began by accepting the conventional four-movement plan although its content was of a kind that expressed and fulfilled itself in a more concentrated and less orthodox span.

The opening movement – a fusion of first movement and scherzo – is one of Sibelius's great syntheses. It moves rather like a series of waves, growing in magnitude and speed. Each upward movement of the wave traces the ascent of an idea to the point of intensification at which it begins to break up, decay, change itself; and each breaking and subsidence of the wave explores the idea in its disfigurement, the contradiction of what it once was. But each antithetical – breaking – motion creates the possibility for the reactivated appearance of the old idea newly formed, for the growth of another wave. And in general each of these motions has more force than the last. The process begins early. The figure that achieves some prominence just before cue C certainly shows traces of the concept of 'second subject'; but it would be a misunderstanding of the dualistic processes of this movement not to see that it is also the first full breaking of the wave: that far from being simply the 'second subject', it is really the 'first subject' (see Ex. 26, i) in the process of contradicting itself. The internal dissolution of the 'first subject' had begun earlier, when its mounting energy had abruptly yielded a minor-mode consequence three bars after cue A; and the 'new' subject is the shape eventually assumed by the music after the nine restless bars that ensue upon this critical moment. The apparently new idea is the 'first' subject in perverted form: little remains intact except the embodied perfect fourth, and even this now tends to move downwards rather than upwards:

Ex. 23

Moreover, the 'first subject's' mellifluous horn instrumentation gives way to the strident woodwind colours of the 'second';

and the syncopation of the 'first' – smooth and easy – reappears in the 'second' in exaggerated distortion. The perversion also affects the underlying accompaniment: the progession of diatonically descending parallel thirds in the 'first subject' becomes the chromatically rising, trembling string accompaniment to the 'second', a sequence containing many diminished triads:

Ex. 24

But the movement thrives on its contradictions. At the beginning of this string tremolo we hardly know whether the new bearing of the music betokens apprehension or awakening excitement, yet from this restlessness will shortly come a new fine certainty, when an emphatic G major appendix terminates the 'second subject'. With this the first wave is complete.

In the midst of development the tonic key erupts, and a splendid *largamente* version of the 'second subject' is declaimed on strings in octaves. Soon after this point, the first movement originally came to a quiet end and the scherzo began at the second cue A[†]. As it is, the transitional passage that begins

[†]   According to Robert Layton's statement in the *Musical Times,* August 1968, p.729.

with a change of key-signature to five sharps brings a truly enhaced reformulation of the opening of the Symphony. The gathering speed and excitement are the pressures that presently make possible the transformation of the principal idea into a dancing ('scherzo') theme, the rebirth of an old theme on a new plane:

Ex. 25

If we are responding to the piece as a festival of change, we can regard as only appropriate the fact that this burst of excitement should take place in a foreign key (B major). E flat is recovered later with a leisurely ostentatiousness culminating in a fanfare-like metamorphosis of the principal motive (Ex. 26, ii) – which then peremptorily reinstates B major. The intrusion of this fanfare theme is dramatic: the links that in mature Sibelius usually explain the genealogy of an apparently fresh idea have been elided here, and it may sound at first like an unrelated theme. But listening closely we can recognize beneath the guise the familiar shape:

Ex. 26

Soon, at cue I, we learn more about this theme. Its history includes not only the original 'first subject' (*x*) but also the original 'second subject' (*y*) as well. The experience of the Symphony is written into the contours of its exfoliations:

Ex. 27

   This 'scherzo' – in so far as one can regard it separately at all – is referable to sonata form: the new ('trio') theme (Ex. 27) is also second subject, and is soon liquidated in the most radical development yet. By the logic of this piece, from the most thorough dissolution will come the most climactic reformulation of the original thematic essence. The final triumphant dash is shot through melodically and harmonically by a tonic apotheosis of the compound movement's thematic source. It is at once coda and quintessential recapitulation, functioning with respect to 'first movement', 'scherzo', and their union as a single entity.
   The ending is *presto;* the first part of the compound movement had been set in a slowish tempo. Oversimplifying a little, one may say that between these poles the movement is a vast accelerando and crescendo. The interesting dichotomy in the movement between the thematic and tonal constituents is a cause – and a consequence – of this. At significant architectonic points the thematic structure is ahead of the tonal. The principal motive is restored (at the first cue E) before the principal key; around the first cue J, the thematic development begins before the main key has been dislodged; thematic recapitulation and the start of the 'scherzo' occur before B major has given way to the tonic; the 'trio' begins a few moments before its key. These disjunctions are part of the sense of acceleration in the movement, of a quickening urgency, as theme leaps repeatedly ahead of its tonal supports, dragging these after it. Tonality

seems to have caught up with theme nine bars after the second cue N, where trumpets announce the recapitulation in the tonic. But both theme and key are now ahead of the structure, because ahead of the full thematic and tonal restoration of the recapitulation. Instead of waiting for the cessation of development, theme and key impatiently begin to recapitulate in its midst. Always in this movement there is no waiting. The music calls forth its own future at the very moment that it becomes realizable.

After this, what can the composer do? The first movement seems self-sufficient; it has carried an argument to a satisfying and triumphant conclusion: this is the problem. Though structurally a free variation movement, the *andante quasi allegretto* has an emotional morphology similar to the first. Through a series of wave-like motions Sibelius attempts to transform it from the sober origins of its opening bars into a dancing, Dionysian whirl. Three times the steady foundation theme issues in buoyant string figures which chase each other along; initially the tempo remains firm, but it soon succumbs to the dynamic propulsion and is worked up in a stretto. And three times, at each ecstatic height, the enthusiasm is abruptly quelled as a dark shape momentarily appears, halting the tempo and deflecting major into minor. This shape is not a form external to the music but an outline which belongs in an obvious way to its own thematic substance. A logical and forceful immanent contradiction in its contexts, it is recognizably the same in each of its fleeting appearances:

Ex. 28

This shadow, this negating implication, is never explored, as the contradictions of the first movement always are. And here is the root of an important difference. The first movement incorporated its antagonisms, made them the very basis of its growth. That does not happen here. The dark consequence of the music temporarily unsettles its flow, prompts it to poignant comment in passing, provokes it (just before cue H) to anguished recollections of the initial thematic urge of the Symphony, pushes it toward tritonally remote regions, and once (near the end) even frustrates it to near extinction of melody. But in every case the effects of the shadow are shaken off as soon as possible so that the music can get back to its simple tunefulness. Finally the music quite abandons its search for the Dionysian state. Instead, it slows down, grows a little whimsical, and ends resignedly.

In a sense, the final *allegro molto* has even less to do with the first movement. True, the two pieces have surface similarities. The second theme of the finale, like the slow peal of a giant carillon, owes its weighty momentum to the accumulated speed of the first theme. Between the two themes, one kind of energy has been transformed into and fulfilled in another – and it is this enjoyment of energy that it shares with the first movement. But in that movement energy develops because of opposites; in this there is no opposition between these themes – not even tonal opposition. The only suggestion of conflict is in the noble coda – alas, too late – where the harmonic clashes are not histrionic but redolent of the pain that has made such triumph possible. Another surface similarity with the first movement is the fact that at times here theme and key are disjunct. But when theme is ahead of key it now has nothing to do with a propulsive, quickening energy; instead it is rhetorical, a static factor in the movement's large architectural design. With reservations the piece might be described as a simplified and tonally deviant sonata form in which the second appearance of the first theme is the development. On the other hand, it might be truer to the spirit of the movement to think of it as basically a simple but unusual ternary structure that describes thematically and tonally a near-perfect symmetry:

A	*B*	:*A*	*A*	*B*	:*B*
E flat		C : C minor	G flat	E flat	E flat
				minor	major

The modulation downwards through a minor third during the second theme (highly effective here, like a sudden shift in the gravitational field) is identically counterbalanced later, the keys of C and G flat being functions of the movement's huge tonal swing a minor third either side of the tonic.

However one listens to the movement, one cannot escape the feeling that it has replaced the fluid, expansive structure of the first movement with a form whose simple contours, repetitiveness and bold symmetry communicate only a sturdy, primitive solidity. The rich, generative complexity has gone.

Symphony No. 6 Op. 104

The Sixth Symphony is in its own, different way, as important a piece of music as the Fourth. The key to the work lies in its opening bars, a passage of quasi-Palestrinian polyphony that is as striking and suggestive as it is surprising in a symphony written between 1917 and 1923: it is surely a powerful and precise symbol of a particular historical period of Western spirituality. Almost as surprising as the occurrence of these bars here is the fact that, once heard, they never return – at least not in their original form; and this is the second key to an understanding of the work. For if we listen closely to what befalls this spiritual symbol we shall hear that it gives way to what, in the light of that spirituality, it will seem proper to speak of as symbols of 'corporeality'. Though there is no record of Sibelius ever having spoken of the Sixth Symphony as an examination of the opposition between the spiritual and the corporeal – or analogously, between the sacred and the secular – we know that he was deeply concerned about the problem of spirituality in his own predominantly secular time. He wrote of this for instance in a letter during a European tour in the autumn of 1911:

Yesterday I heard Bruckner's B flat Symphony and it moved me to tears. For a long time afterwards I was completely enraptured. What a strangely profound spirit, formed by religiousness. And this profound religiousness we have abolished in our own country as something no longer in harmony with our time.

Among the characteristics most specific to the 'Palestrinian' opening, we notice its homogeneous texture and its sense of not belonging to worldly time, which it derives mainly from the apparent endlessness and the free rhythms of its lines, as well as from its not being rooted in tonality (it is modal, in a Dorian D). Also worth noticing is the cell of four descending notes, variously woven into the texture; this is the thematic germinating motive of the entire symphony, and it can easily be traced throughout. The modal polyphony soon begins to break down: first through the way thematic lines spontaneously separate themselves from the polyphonic texture, slowly condensing into recognizable figures around a common metrical basis, and then tonally, just before letter B. These thirty-odd opening bars vanish for ever; but the Symphony will in a sense be an effort to recover, or reappropriate, them in another form – in terms that acknowledge, and transcend, all subsequent contradictory developments. Implications reveal themselves rapidly. The dissonance before cue B picks up the two accidentals that have appeared in forms suggested by *musica ficta,* and throws C sharp in the woodwind and lower strings against the C (natural) major chord of the brass, a minor explosion that finally frees the new system of thematic and harmonic organization. Now the music is outspokenly homophonic: the old *melos* is replaced by something close to 'tune', with accompaniment; now also there is a regular metrical beat; and tonality, which soon settles in C major. Gone is the quality of wholeness; instead there are merely fragments, which here seem able only to fly about without cohesion. The rich spirituality has also gone, and in its place is what we may call an exuberant, secular banality. This is, and must be, delightful. But we shall not fully understand what this reversal means – what its true force and content are – until the fourth movement. We can know nothing yet of the special kind of violence to which it may lead. We must enjoy the distinct and positive qualities of this healthy secularity: its gaiety and freshness, its radiant open-air simplicity.

In its tonal phase the music inevitably generates tonal contradiction. Abruptly we are in G flat, as far as we could be from C. We must be careful how we speak of music whose sections are as self-evidently its own, and as rational, as here. What we have now is not the 'development' so much as a section in which the music is developing. The previous section – expository, if you like – did not have a 'second subject' so much as a cluster of motives that were explicitly the exfoliation of possibilities inherent in the polyphonic beginning. The new section dissolves the distinction (made in the 'exposition') between polyphony and homophony, and replaces them with a homogeneous texture in which neither is truly represented. The result is a kind of toccata. The 'tune' element is loosened horizontally, while the polyphonic element is tightened vertically into rigid, patterned symmetries.

Because of this texture, and because the music fixes itself almost pointillistically around unrelated triads, this section cumulatively achieves a curious sensation of stillness, despite its restless activity. It comes to seem not like a busy motion through time, but the prolongation of a single moment of time, expanded and examined in its texture. Time freezes. But these qualities, textural homogeneity and timelessness, are among those which belong to the 'spiritual' opening of the Symphony; and their reappearance here is the first partial recreation of that opening in terms which equally derive from its secular – or corporeal – antithesis. But it cannot last. Tune stirs again, from the region of B minor – logically, because B minor, with two basic sharps, is a late tonal implication of the accidentals F sharp and C sharp heard in the early stages of the movement. The music aims for the original D Dorian, however; and there, picking up its thematic origins at the very point where they began to appear as finite melody, quite simply recomposes its subsequent evolution. But in place of the earlier fragmentation, all now moves with single-minded purpose and assurance, impelled by the firm internal pulse of a body whose parts function in tune with each other. And unthought-of thematic possibilities are also discovered – particularly the ecstatic dance-like passage after cue I, incarnated in iridescent textures. The reason for so much regeneration is clear. Just as this whole section's momentum and much of its *moto perpetuo* activity derive from the 'development', so its new felicitousness is made possible by that section's spiritual experience. After this, the eerie and disruptive conclusion is alarming. We had not thought so destructive a potential could be entailed by this music; only later shall we fully understand its source and consequence. Now it undermines the climactic C major and brings the movement to an end, dropping it at the final moment of decline into the Dorian D of the opening.

The slow movement seems to be concerned with the secular in its lyrical aspect. The three thematic constituents of its subject matter – wind chords, a halting string melody, and sequential scale passages – derive in various ways from the fractured conclusion of the first movement. And they contradict one another – not only thematically, but tonally as well – in their restless pulling towards and against each other. The movement has three settings of this thematic complex, each more full and rounded, more coherent, than the last. But the essential experience never changes: there is an upward-sweeping approach to the theme, a fleeting moment of exquisite poise, and then a falling away and disintegration. Each time the music rises towards the theme through D, and falls back onto it afterwards. So D, which in the first movement was an area of modal fragility and finally of defeat, participates here but only as a subordinate region – as a dominant, and as the extremeties of a trajectory. These are the consequences of the first movement, for D. Tonality, throughout this Symphony, is wonderfully symbolic.

The three settings are three attempts to find poise and stability – to find stillness – all of which fail. Now, four bars beyond cue F, Sibelius asks us to make an important discovery with him: namely that failure itself has the potential to release a new idea. The idea is a tiny thematic particle

Ex. 29

and a generating point so inspired that when it abruptly uncovers its possibilities we are astonished. Once more the music suddenly freezes. The former striving has given place to a poised fixity, a passage incorporating the tiny particle and centred on slowly alternating extended dominant forms of F and D (again). Nothing had prepared us for this. It is a demonstration of the objective presence of an antithetical mode of being, beneath the most concealing of superficial appearances. But the specific content of this alternative mode is what counts. It is transfixed, achieving immobility at the expense of all harmony and most melody, and seeking textural homogeneity – all rather like the developmental section of the first movement. In the 'failure' of secular song the music has found a spiritual inwardness. The passage attains rare qualities near its end, going beyond the parallel with the first movement, opening out into a final rapturous, multi-layered, polyphonic and polyrhythmic concordance – and all in the rarefied air of an extended dominant of D flat major.

The central movements may perhaps be regarded as belonging together. They appear to be involved with the secular world, in two archetypal musical manifestations. We have had secular song, and now the scherzo presents the secular to us in its most corporeal aspect – as *dance*. Like the slow movement, like even the first movement, it has a telling experience, a revelation, at its centre. Nowhere in the piece does the speed change, the propulsive reflex lag. There is a scherzo but no trio. There is, however, a different section after about cue B, where the dash, the pulse, is kept but the energy curiously redirected. It is a transformation of which we become aware only after some bars, and it is this: the music is transfixed upon an immovable centre point (made up of an implacable rhythmic figure and a protracted – 'suspended' – dominant harmony) about which it begins slowly to revolve. The complementary dance-groups of woodwind and strings swing alternately into and out of view, their partnership reflected in the continuous, circular, tetratonic canon on violins and cellos. As the stamp of the dance mounts, a simple, affecting pentatonic chant is sounded, alone at first, then in canon between flute and harp,

completing a radiant and sonorous cacophony. What happens
here is that precisely through the cumulative corporeal assertion a strange trance-like state of suspended momentum – a
point of rest outside of time – has been forced into being. And
the high degree of textural homogeneity, and the incipient
(canonic) polyphony, relate the section to others that have
partially recreated the original spirituality. It is a state of being
that does not – cannot – last long. With a shock the music slips
back to its former condition. But later the trance-like condition
is reattained; and it is remarkable that where this state broke
down the first time under the violent blow of an F sharp minor
chord it is now destroyed by a C sharp minor chord, F sharp and
C sharp being the two accidentals associated with the decay of
modal polyphony at the very beginning of the Symphony.

The first movement began with spirituality and allowed
corporeal traits to exfoliate in opposition to it; then showed the
secular realm rediscovering something of its antithesis and
growing relatively more whole as a result. But the sensibility of
of the opening was lost; and the middle movements, asserting
the corporeal world, reached spiritual insight both by default
of secularity (in the slow movement) and the extreme assertion
of it (in the scherzo). The finale begins (in C major) with what
the Symphony has learnt: that somehow, sometimes, these
divided modes of being can be united. It starts with a kind of
chorale – the recreation of the spiritual in an historical form
that already accommodates some secularity. We know the
chorale-like character by (say) the square phrases separated by
fermatae and the quasi-chorale cadences; the simple, bold,
singable lines making use of 'popular' elements, grounded in a
harmonic setting in which all voices basically aspire to a
melodic interest:

Ex. 30

The antiphonal technique only emphasizes the spiritual origins of the passage: as happened with the quasi-Palestrinian music at the start of the Symphony, this symbolic representation soon leads beyond itself, in typical Sibelian fashion extrapolating motives charged with new implications. But between the motives and the actual realization of what they imply, most links are elided: we move suddenly to an energetic dance, of quasi-folk character. The contrast plays off sacred against secular in a way that dramatically poses the central issue of the Symphony. With an unfailing sense of his whole purpose, Sibelius has put this dance section in D – the region of the 'Palestrinian' beginning. Across three movements this fact binds these two deeply contrasted sections together, forces us to see them as having the same source. And the next revelation is horrific. The dance has a tendency to work itself up, in each of its three sections, into a state of some excitement; but the third section at last reveals the true violence bequeathed to the secular realm through the fragmentation of sensibility into the spiritual and the corporeal. Totally disfigured, the dance becomes all whirling, frenzied violence that destroys tonality and issues in an incoherent scream.

It is one of the profound ironies of the Symphony that what once seemed pure delight should now reveal the countenance of terror. And it is no accident that the climax falls heavily upon B minor. That key was the turning-point of the 'development' in the first movement, just as it is of the developmental extension of the dance subject in this. Since that key has hardly been present since then, and certainly not as a rooted tonic, its occurrence here is a strong allusion to that spot in the tranquil first movement: it enables us still more clearly to understand the present violence as precisely that which was concealed by the first movement. This violence was implicit in the original split in sensibility; and the full, final admission and comprehension of this fact is one of the   achievements of the Symphony.

What ensues is the climax of the work and its moment of greatest genius. No mere statement of the antithesis to this barbaric outcry will now suffice: we have reached the end point in a long demonstration that the opposites are linked, that they contain and generate each other. Think of trying to answer this outrage even with its extreme antithesis, the 'Palestrinian' beginning. It would be absurd, if only because we know that the one has led to the other; and we saw that this fact was stressed by their both being in D. So here the Symphony does something new. The return of the 'chorale' theme is agitated, anxious. Soon we know why. Something is happening to it; it is changing itself in its very essence, and after only a few bars it offers itself in a full re-formulation. It is still recognizably the 'chorale' melody, but the specific nature of the transformation is this: *the chorale has learnt to dance.* It has tapped the violent energies of the preceding section, redeeming them by a synthesis which is greater than either of the components. Out of the destruction has come a new whole, a unity of the spiritual and the corporeal:

Ex. 31

Ever a rationalist, Sibelius lets us – makes us – hear this process taking place: it is an astonishing experience, evidence of the way the sonata procedures of late Beethoven had penetrated Sibelius's thinking. Once again key is significant. The new section is not in C major, the key of the opening of the movement and the one we might have expected; this tonality

has been superseded and will not appear again. Consistent with
the fact that the music has surpassed its contradictions, it
inhabits a place where tonal and modal tendencies mix freely.
Here it is in F – but an F replete with fruitful, innervating
tensions from, for example, major and minor, Lydian and
Mixolydian.

But a question that has loomed since the beginning of the
Symphony persists. Has the original spirituality been fully
recreated? As if to show us that it has, Sibelius slows down the
dancing, allows the music to reveal its deepest mind. What we
hear is an apotheosis both of the movement's main theme
(through a free mirror deployment of it) and of the Symphony's
basic four-note germ motive. It is a wonderful utterance, and
one which in its resonant string character, its marked
polyphonic interest, its expressive linear continuity and flow,
unmistakably recalls the very opening of the Symphony. It does
so also by reverting to that section's modal D – but with tonal
and chromatic differences that speak for all that the music has
experienced since then. A modal-tonal-chromatic complex, the
music takes in as much of modulation as the equal-tempered
scale will allow, stretching itself from F major all the way to F
flat, but wrapping itself round with modality and closing the
Symphony in a modal D. This fully regenerated spirituality is
no simplistic return to 'Palestrina', though in a sense it
certainly 'comprehends' the original polyphony as part of its
experience. But we must hear also that the music of this
regenerated, unified sensibility is finer and richer than that of
the opening of the first movement. The 'Palestrina' has gone,
like its secular opposite, but we have arrived at this instead.
And from the point of view of this music we can have no wish to
return to any earlier world. It is a vision of a stage beyond the
dualities endured by this Symphony.

Symphony No. 7 in C Op. 105

Sibelius began his symphonic career by trying to give
symphonic thought a new life by liberating it from outmoded

form. His final Symphony (1918-24) is his most extreme and consistent demonstration of the coming to life of symphonic thought outside of old structures. This Symphony finally abolishes the old multi-movement scheme, and with it the organized sequence of separate forms. It abandons the orthodox succession of tempi, the conventional techniques of obtaining contradiction, of thematic forming, contrast, and development. All this and much besides – a great part of it, as we have seen, already accomplished in the first six symphonies. Unlike probably any one-movement symphony before it, this work is not just a complex modification of traditional techniques, not (say) a mere linking or even intertwining of several movements into what looks like one. Rather, negating these techniques, it is a single, indivisible movement; and yet everywhere there are traces of those techniques and of the old pattern of movements. That is a paradox which can be understood only by seeing this Symphony as a unity wrought out of all that it has abolished. Which provokes another thought: that the Seventh Symphony, by the very fact of its being a revolutionary work, is also a deeply traditional one; its concern is to attend to the essence of the symphonic tradition rather than to its appearances. Perhaps these were subtleties which the composer did not expect others easily to understand; for possibly fearing wholesale misunderstanding, he offered the piece at its first performance under the loose name of 'Fantasia Sinfonica'.

But the technical accomplishment of the work has no real value distinct from its total accomplishment. Sibelius has not invented a new form, which can now be separated and used again like a mould. Form, if it is alive, is specific: it is the way a particular work realizes itself. And form here is important because it is *this* marvellously apt way of bringing the Seventh Symphony into being; because by expressing itself this way – and no other – the Seventh Symphony expresses itself with perfect precision. Sibelius always wanted to be clear. And he is clear here as perhaps nowhere else: this is what we mean – or ought to mean – by good 'form'.

The first three bars of the Symphony present the work's basic urge and its fundamental contradiction. The ascending scale moves with increasing power and sureness: it appears quite unchallenged. Then, without seeming to intend to come to an end, suddenly it is drastically cut off; and the aftermath is played out chromatically. The long and deeply beautiful polyphonic passage that follows after a few bars clarifies the initial urge. Apparently, the music here is beyond the reach of time and change: a piece of quasi-Palestrinian polyphony like the beginning of the Sixth Symphony, it is atemporal in the sense in which that opening was atemporal. Besides, so continuous and open-ended is its *melos* that it seems to hold a guarantee that it can extend itself endlessly. And yet it does finally disintegrate, around cue D. Thus in the space of a few bars the Symphony is twice surprised – twice defeated – by its own inherent finitude and inevitable changeability.

At first the music registers the existence of its own negating principle only symptomatically: it reacts, with pain. But this principle has its fingerprints, and we soon learn to recognize them. The continuous scale that opens the Symphony is broken off through the unexpected treatment of the note D as a leading note to E flat, supported by A flat and C flat; D is thus tritonally contradicted by an A flat minor triad:

Ex. 32

A couple of quick reappearances of this semitonal interception develop and enhance its cadential nature, its power to defy endlessness, and deflect the music onto a new course:

Ex. 33

It even swerves the music into A flat around bar 18, thus extending a tonal characteristic first shown in Ex. 32. In the polyphonic passage a different emphasis of phrasing throws into relief a new aspect (*y*) of Ex. 33:

Ex. 34

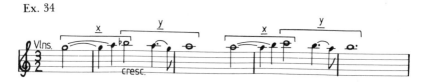

The flow of the music is sufficiently strong around cue C to withstand such attempts to deflect it, but only until its culmination in the noble trombone theme. Then its polyphonic 'endlessness' is terminated. The process is inaugurated by a line with familiar characteristics, including the clear presence of an A flat chord (indicated in the example by an asterisk) as the superstructure of a minor subdominant seventh chord, F-E flat-C-A flat, which functions as a species of interrupted cadence:

Ex. 35

The music breaks up into wailing fragments that are not any longer the culmination of what has gone before, but the consequences of – and indeed the agents of – the decay:

Ex. 36

The music begins a long struggle in the developmental explorations which start before cue F. Here it suffers to the full the pain of its own basic contradiction. And development is now almost continuous – but for three interruptions – until the final pages of the Symphony. It is important to notice that it is associated with motion, that is to say, with a heightened sense of the passing of time: the tempo quickens as the struggle begins. But the adagio had been able to seem so monumentally slow as to be motionless; after all, this apparent condition of not being subject to time had been one pole of the duality. So it is wonderfully apt that with the music's full immersing of itself in contradiction, and its full experiencing of finitude, a sense of time – of a quickening of pulse – should enter the music. The development tries to clarify the contradiction, perhaps, one may even say, to understand it. In recollection of the opening bars, a scale is played upwards; though it is in C minor, the fact that it reaches A natural – the ascending melodic-minor form – indicates that it would continue in the same direction. But instead it is suddenly dragged down, rhythmically distorted into a triplet, and replaced by the now familiar negating idea:

Ex. 37

In reaching A natural the scale had at least avoided A flat, the tonal symbol of the negating principle; but the failure of its next upward run brings down a shower of A flat minor (notated as G sharp) upon it. Later on, the power of the negative to intercept semitonally, deflect, and cadence – all of which operations we have already seen – is more fully explored. The rising scale is now not only prevented from completing its course, but also deflected into another key through the treatment of the ascending-sixth degree as a leading note:

Ex. 38

These phrases alternate with such developments of the negating idea as:

Ex. 39

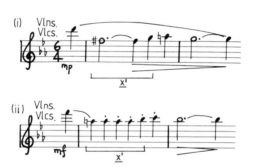

In this passage, and in the *vivacissimo* (with its residual scherzo function) that follows, the semitone so characteristic of the negative is experienced in two important harmonic roles. Much use is made of it to clinch the abrupt movements of the tonal root in rapid sequences (already suggested by Ex. 39); and it creates constellations of harmonic and tonal structures separated by a semitone (such as that between the dominant of C, G, and its Neapolitan – A flat again).

The first return of the trombone theme is premature; it 'fails' because the development still has much to clarify. The music has merely pacified the negative into the heaving string lines, not comprehended it: perhaps that is why the disintegration of the theme is so violent. The precipitous arrival of the symbolic A flat minor (again notated as G sharp) is foretold by the moaning horn lines, a fusion of phrases y and y^1 from Ex. 36, centred on that very same A flat. Abruptly we are plunged back into development; the tonal foothold is slipping semitonally downwards and will not stop until it reaches the affirmative C, the home-key of the Symphony.

Then at last the music is in a position to see the poles of the dualism for what they are. As so often in the later stages of a Sibelius symphony this new lucidity means that what was formerly expressed only symptomatically, as an immanent contradiction, can now be formulated objectively, as a manifest contradiction. Here its expression takes the form of a sonata structure. The negative principle, grasped and identified for what it is, is objectified as second subject; its shape owes much to the main experience of the 'scherzo':

Ex. 40

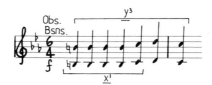

to which it gives a still more precise definition:

Ex. 41

The C major first subject identifies itself, chiefly by allusion, with the polyphonic passage and trombone theme; but it is not until the sonata development that we understand why those

early symbols have so transformed themselves. Then all is made
clear. By this re-formulation the music's positives make
themselves much more accessible to the negative principle, and
thereby open themselves to an acceptance of it. This is particularly strongly suggested by the easy intermingling of the
opposites in Ex. 42: here a phrase from the first subject is
followed by the second subject, then the two appear almost to
coalesce:

Ex. 42

After this there is no reason why the positives should any longer
inhabit only C, and the negative principle other areas; as if to
prove it, the subjects recapitulate in reversed tonal situations.
The first acknowledges the alien area of E flat (the note to
which D in the rising scale passage was deflected in the third
bar of the Symphony) and the second C minor. It is only one of
the features of the greatness of this Symphony that the music's
acceptance in the sonata-allegro of a relatively rapid and stable
pulse – a symbol of time – coincides exactly with the music's
clarification and acceptance of its own inescapable finitude.
The two are of course intimately related.

Sonata recapitulation leads to a coda-like passage (*vivace*)
which seems to gather to a point all the negative energies that
have been at work in the Symphony. This coda embodies
harmonically the semitonal character of the negating principle

in a long sequence of Neapolitan relationships; it is an extension of the sonata's second subject; and in appearance and by
virtue of the suddenly quicker tempo it outspokenly recalls the
scherzo, of which it is a sharper, more streamlined formulation.
The passage confirms that the negative has been precisely
located, and summarizes its force; and it does more than that.
By closely associating itself with the scherzo it also allows us to
compare what happened then – when the negative was suppressed by a premature return of the trombone theme – with
what happens now – when the trombone theme returns in a
new relationship to the negative.

A way to explain this difference is to say that the negative
symbols, instead of opposing the trombone theme and all
associated with it, now enter constitutively into it. As a result,
neither exists as it did before; both have been superseded by a
new whole which 'knows' but transcends the original conflict.
The negative belongs to the very dynamic of the final affirmation, from the moment of the long dominant approach to the
trombone theme:

Ex. 43

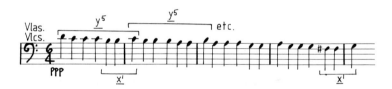

But it is what happens after this moment that is most
wonderful of all. The music from the beginning of the trombone theme until beyond cue Z is a recomposition of the first
statement of that theme and its subsequent fragmentation; as
such it is another comparison which makes possible our
participation in the wisdom the music has acquired. This time
one cannot speak of a breakdown, though certainly the original
negative traits (for instance, Exs. 35 and 36) are present. The
music arrives once more at the same point where formerly the
trombone theme began to disintegrate; but now it takes this

point as the very source of the energy by which it moves. The moment is nevertheless an anticlimax, coming at the very height of the music's aspiration; few moments in music are as tragic as this. Yet the Symphony seems to welcome the anguish, allowing it to enrich the current of the music and deepen the bed upon which it flows. Certainly, this moment is one that taxes most fully its power to unite opposites into a sustained flow; and yet from it the music draws the capacity to carry itself to a climax which comprehends and depends upon everything that has preceded it. In so doing the music demonstrates that its own 'limitation' – the finitude, the changeability that has menaced it since the beginning – need not inevitably be a weakness but can become the very realm of its strength. The Symphony's final utterance is its quintessence: two slow and passionate gestures, one a movement from D to C, the other from B to C. The first is the opening of the trombone theme, the second the kernel of the negative symbol; and they unite in a harmonious fusion that affirms the conclusion of the Symphony.

'Symphony No. 8'

The Seventh Symphony was completed in 1924; *Tapiola* in 1925. An Eighth Symphony was repeatedly promised, but if it ever existed at all – as seems likely – then the composer destroyed it. He died in 1957, having produced nothing of any importance, and hardly any music at all, for thirty years. How might this be explained?

Above all Sibelius was a symphonist. He wrote symphonies because this was the musical style that, innately as well as historically, had the deepest affinity with the kind of liberation struggle in which Finland was involved. All his published symphonies were conceived within earshot of the struggle, even though the last two were actually worked out in the years immediately after independence. Now the gaining of constitutional freedom did not solve all Finland's problems. The experience of unity in the face of the aggressor was replaced by domestic disunity founded upon explosive class tensions. We can see how this situation posed for Sibelius, in an extremely acute form, a conflict between two radically different ways of thinking: as a private citizen there was the logic of his sectarian interests, which asked that he defend his way of life against further change; and there was the logic of the symphonic thinker which demanded that he admit the contradictions and strive for a restructuring of the whole. We know how he chose. By 1930 Sibelius was ready to write a choral march for the Lapua movement, which (according to the historian J. Hampden Jackson) was a conspiracy of capitalist interests to bring about a form of Fascist dictatorship in Finland.†

But the testimony of his long silence is that Sibelius's espousal of partisan interests did not satisfy the demands of his artistic conscience, which had always expressed and been excited by the conditions for change in a given totality. These were the inspirational sources of Sibelius's art, which, when he spoke of them, he plainly identified with Finland. He maintained that to lose touch with these sources – with Finland as an idealized totality – would cut him off directly from the roots of his art. Such knowledge evidently did not prevent him from taking the stance that he did. The choice was his own, and it committed him to sterility.

SELECT BIBLIOGRAPHY

ABRAHAM, Gerald, *A Hundred Years of Music*, London 1964.

ABRAHAM, Gerald, *Sibelius: A Symposium*, London 1952.

ADORNO, Theodor W., and Horkheimer, Max, *Dialectic of Enlightenment* (trans. John Cumming), New York 1972.

ADORNO, Theodor W., *Philosophy of Modern Music* (trans. Anne G. Mitchell and Wesley V. Blomster), New York 1973.

ADORNO, Theodor W., *Prisms* (trans. Samuel and Shierry Weber), London 1967.

ARNOLD, Elliot, *Finlandia: the Story of Sibelius*, New York 1941.

---

† *Finland*, London, 1940, p.156

BALLANTINE, Christopher, 'Beethoven, Hegel and Marx', *Music Review*, Feb. 1972, Vol. 33 No.1, pp.34-46, reproduced in this book as Chapter II.

CARDUS, Neville, *A Composers Eleven*, London 1958.

CHERNIAVSKY, David, 'Sibelius and Finland', *Musical Times*, 1950.

EKMAN, Karl, *Jean Sibelius: His Life and Personality*, London 1936.

GOLLWITZER, Heinz, *Europe in the Age of Imperialism*, London 1969.

GRAY, Cecil, *Sibelius*, London 1934.

HANNIKAINEN, Ilmari, *Sibelius and the Development of Finnish Music* (trans. Aulis Nopsanen), London 1949.

HOBSBAWM, Eric, *The Age of Revolution : 1789-1848*, London 1962.

JACKSON, J. Hampden, *Finland*, London (rev.) 1940.

JOHNSON, Harold E., *Sibelius*, London 1960.

JUTIKKALA, Eino, *A History of Finland*, London 1962.

LAMBERT, Constant, *Music Ho!*, London 1966.

LAYTON, Robert, *Sibelius*, London 1965.

LUKÁCS, Georg, *The Historical Novel* (trans. Hannah and Stanley Mitchell), London 1962.

MARCUSE, Herbert, *Negations: Essays in Critical Theory* (trans. Jeremy J. Shapiro), London 1968.

MARCUSE, Herbert, *One Dimensional Man : The Ideology of Industrial Society*, London 1968.

MARCUSE, Herbert, *Reason and Revolution : Hegel and the Rise of Social Theory*, London 1941.

MEAD, W. R., *Finland*, London 1968.

NEWMARCH, Rosa, *Jean Sibelius : A Short History of a Long Friendship*, London 1944.

NIETZSCHE, Friedrich, *The Birth of Tragedy* (trans. Francis Golffing), New York 1956.

PARMET, Simon, *The Symphonies of Sibelius* (trans. Kingsley A. Hart), London 1959.

TANZBERGER, Ernst, *Jean Sibelius: Eine Monographie*, Wiesbaden 1962.

TÖRNE, Bengt de, *Sibelius : a Close-Up*, London 1937.

TOVEY, Donald Francis, *Essays in Musical Analysis* (Vol. II), London 1956.

WESTRUP, Jack, 'Jean Sibelius : born 8 December 1865, died 20 September 1957', *Musical Times*, Nov. 1957, Vol. 98 No. 1377, pp. 601-3.

WOOD, Ralph W., 'Sibelius's Use of Percussion', *Music and Letters*, Vol. XXIII, 1942, p.10 ff.

Index

Abert, Anna Amalie & *Don Giovanni* 60
Adorno, Theodor 22, 27-8, 118, 121
  Beethoven xvii
  experimental music 121, 107
  function of art 121
  Mozart 49
  Mozart string quartets 118
  neutralized consciousness xvii-xviii
  social analysis of music xv-xviii
  thesis art 109-110
Antal, Frederick art & society 23
Aristophanes art & reality 12
Aristotle 123-4
  art & reality 12
  non-Aristotelian drama & music 133-4
Arnold, Matthew 'West London' 78-80

Bach, C. P. E. 38
  & the bourgeoisie 93
Bach, J. S. 9, 39-40, 78-80
  Art of Fugue 93
  Bachian principle 33-4
  bourgeois-popular music 93
  function of music x
  fugues 47
  & hit tunes 100
  & Charles Ives 78-80, 85

& social structures 5
Balzac, Honoré de 26, 33
  art & reality 12-13
Barthes, Roland 11
Beatles, The 96-7
  & Marcuse 96-7
Beethoven, Ludwig van x-xiii, xvii, 9, 30-4, 93, 134-40, 157, 169, 184
  & Adorno xvii
  & Willian Blake xii-xiii
  & contradiction xi, 141-2
  function of music x
  French Revolution 19, 31-4, 47-8, 134-6
  & Charles Ives 78
  last works 93
  & Marx 43-8
  & Sibelius x-xiii, 157, 169
  & social structures 5
  sonata principle 134-6
  Fifth Symphony 9, 40-2, 46, 78, 85, 146
  Seventh Symphony 42-3
  Ninth Symphony 39, 46
Benjamin, Walter art & aura 114-6
  art & technology 108-9
  audience participation 122-3, 131
  changes in art 113-4
  dialectic in art 128
  'dramatic laboratory' 127-8

197

epic theatre 124
epic theatre & new technical
forms 130
& experimental music 107, 126
film 126, 131
function of art 109-10
Jeztzeiten xvii-xviii
theatre as apparatus 113-4
Berger, John 11
Berlioz, Hector 9
Boulex, Pierre 95, 129-30
& the avant-garde 94
avant-garde music 129
& Morton Feldman 130
& Stockhausen 129-30
Brahms, Johannes Second
Symphony 85
Brecht, Bertolt alienation 122
art & ritual 116
audience participation 123-4
epic theatre 108-9, 113-4, 122,
124
epic theatre & new technical
forms 130-1
& experimental music 107
Galileo 127
'rational' entertainment 127-8
scientific approach to art 127-8
theatre as apparatus 114
& *Ulysses* 131
Breton, André 114
objective chance 121
Britten, Benjamin 96
Brophy, Brigid & *Die Entführung
aus dem Serail* 64
Bruckner, Anton & Charles Ives
85
& Sibelius 177-8
B flat Symphony 177-8
Burney, Charles definition of
music ix-x
Busoni, Ferrucio & *Don Giovanni*
61
Butor, Michel & *Finnegan's Wake*
131

Cage, John 128-30
& art 111
experimental music 124-6,
128-30
& Morton Feldman 130
music & passivity 117-8
& Stockhausen 129-30
4' 33' 95
Cardew, Cornelius 118-9
experimental improvisation 125
experimental music 129
The Great Learning 112-3
improvisation 118-9
Memories of You 121-2
Scratch Orchestra 112-3
Carter, Elliott & Ives 89
Cassiodorus 2
Chailley, Jacques *Die Zauberflöte*
56
Chase, Gilbert theory of
musicology 16
Comte, Auguste 138-9
Cone, Edward T. function of
analysis 20
Cowper, William 78-9

Dada 114-5, 120-2, 128
& experimental music 120-1
Debussy, Claude & experimental
music 121
Descartes, René 21
Dewan, Edmond & Alvin Lucier
125
Duchamps, Marcel *Mona Lisa* 122
Dvořák, Anton *New World
Symphony* 85
Dylan, Bob xii, 96-7, 101-6
& The Band 101, 104-6
Blonde on Blonde 102-3
& country & western 104-5
'Here with you' 105
'I'll be your baby tonight' 103
'I shall be free—No. 10' 102
John Wesley Harding 103
& Marcuse 96-7

Nashville Skyline 101-6
'One more night' 106
'Sad-eyed lady of the lowlands' 102-3
'Tell me that it isn't true' 105-6

Eisler, Hanns art & technology 108
Éluard, Paul 120
  & Apollinaire 120
Emerson, Ralph Waldo & Charles Ives 78
van Eycks & art & economic history 23

Feldman, Morton 130
  & Boulez 130
  & Cage 130
Freud, Sigmund dreams 74, 90

Galileo & Brecht 127
God 93
Goethe, Johann Wolfgang von art & reality 12
Goldmann, Lucien dialectics 21-2
  specialization 7

Hamlet art & reality 12
Harrison, F. L. function of musicology 15
  music & society 18
Haydn, Joseph 32-3, 39-40
  & the dialectic 45
  & Hegel 38
  sonata principle 134
Handel, George Frideric art & reality 13
  music & society
Hegel, Georg Wilhelm Friederich 32-48, 135-8
  art & reality 12
  & dialectics & sonata xi, 32-40, 135-8
  & Haydn 38
  & Mozart 38

Hobsbawm, Eric academic history 14
Hoggart, Richard problems of language 11
Hood, Mantle theory of music history 16

Ives, Charles 72-91
  & Matthew Arnold 78-80
  & Bach 78-80, 85
  & Beethoven's Fifth Symphony 78, 85
  & Brahms's Second Symphony 85
  & Bruckner 85
  & William Cowper 78-9
  Central Park in the Dark 87-8
  & Emerson 78
  & dialectics 73-4
  & the dream 75-6
  Fourth of July 90
  & Lowell Mason 78-82
  & Santayana 83
  First Piano Sonata 85
  Concord Sonata 77-8, 83
  String Quartet No. 2 76-8, 85-6
  Second Symphony 85
  Fourth Symphony 80-2
  & the *New World* Symphony 85
  & Tchaikovsky's Sixth Symphony 85
  & Thoreau 78
  & *Tristan und Isolde* 85
  & *Die Walküre* 85
  Washington's Birthday 88-90
  'West London' 78-80
  & 'Westminster Chimes' 77
  & David Wooldridge 78

Jackson, J. Hampden Lapua movement 195
Jacobi, Jolande dreams 90
Jenny, Hans & Alvin Lucier 125
  The Queen of the South 125

Jones, Gareth Stedman positivistic
view of history 14

Kerman, Joseph *Cosi fan tutte* 55
Kierkegaard, Soren & Mozart 57
  & *Le Nozze di Figaro* 64
Knepler, Georg theory of music
history 15

Lang, Paul Henry music & society
17-18
Lapua movement 195
Lautrémont, Comte de 114
Layton, Robert & Sibelius
Symphony No. 5 172
Lee, Frankie 103
Lehár, Franz entertainment music 93-4
Lippman, Edward A. musical
research 16
Lucier, Alvin & Edmond Dewan
125
  I Am Sitting in a Room 116-7, 125
  & Hans Jenny 125
  Music for Solo Performer 125
  & Michael Nyman 125
  *The Only Talking Machine of Its
  Kind in the World* 117
  Quasimodo the Great Lover 125
  The Queen of the South 125
  Vespers 125
Lukács, Georg art & realism 23-8

Marcuse, Herbert 96-7
  art & the bourgeoisie 20
  & The Beatles 96-7
Mason, Lowell 78-82
  'Bethany' 80-2
  'Watchman' 81-2
Marx, Karl 6-7, 24, 43-8
  & Beethoven 43-8
Merleau-Ponty, Maurice 30, 36-7
Metzger, Heinz-Klaus
experimental music 124
Mozart, Wolfgang Amadeus 32-3,
39-40, 49-71, 93

  & Adorno 49, 118
  Cosi fan tutte 49-50, 52, 54-5, 62-
  3, 66-7
  & the dialectic 45, 57-65
  Don Giovanni 49-50, 52-4, 57-62,
  64, 66-7
  & the Enlightment 68-70
  Die Entführung aus dem Serail 49-
  51, 64-6
  & Hegel 38
  & Freemasons 69-70
  & Kierkegaard 57
  last works 93
  Le Nozze di Figaro 49-52, 64, 101
  & 'reality' 50-7
  & 'reconciliation & forgiveness'
  65-70
  & Charles Rosen 57
  & Alfred Schutz 59-60
  sonata principle 134
  string quartets 118
  Symphony No. 40 in G minor 9
  Die Zauberflöte 49-50, 55-7, 63-4,
  66

Neuhaus, Max *Puplic Supply* 110-
111
  Telephone Access 110-111
Nietzsche, Friederich 138-9
  & Sibelius 143
Nyman, Michael & Alvin Lucier
125
  Scratch Orchestra 112

Offenbach, Jacques entertainment
music 93-4

Palestrina, Giovanni Pierluigi da
184-5
  & Sibelius 184-5

Rank, Otto & Don Giovanni 53
von Ranke, Leopold 14
Reader's Digest *Music for You* 97-
101

Resnais, Alain 56
Reti, Rudolph & Beethoven's
 Ninth Symphony 39
 & sonata & contradiction 34-6
Reich, Steve 127
Robinson, Eric *Music for You* 99-
 101
Rodgers and Hammerstein
 entertainment music 93-4
Rolling Stones, The 96-7
Rosen, Charles & Mozart 57
 & *Don Giovanni* 59, 61-2
 & eighteenth-century comedy
 68
Rossini, Gioacchino
 entertainment music 93-4
Rzewski, Frederic *Free Soup* 111-2
 Les Moutons de Panurge 112
 Sound Pool 112

Sartre, Jean-Paul 46
Santayana, George 83
Sanguineti, Eduardo 131
Shaw, George Bernard & *Don
 Giovanni* 53
Schiller, Friederich art & reality
 13
 The Artists 13
Schoenberg, Arnold & art 92
 art-for-an-elite 94
 & experimental music 121
Schubert, Franz 101
 last works 93
 & Romanticism & the dialectic
 136-7
 song-tune 137
Schutz, Alfred & Mozart 59-60
Seeger, Charles theory of
 musicology 16-17
Sibelius, Jean & Beethoven x-xiii,
 157, 169, 184
 & Bruckner 177-8
 & Finland 194-5
 & imperialism 138-9
 & Nietzsche 143

 & Palestrina 184-5
 Symphony No. 1 140-6
 Symphony No. 2 146-54, 160
 Symphony No. 3 154-60
 Symphony No. 4 160-70
 Symphony No. 5 169-77
 Symphony No. 6 177-85
 Symphony No. 7 185-94
 Symphony No. 8 194-5
 & symphony & the dialectic x-
 xi, 139-40
Stockhausen, Karlheinz & avant-
 garde music 128-30
 & the avant-garde 94
 & Boulez 129-30
 & Cage 129-30
 Momente 128
 & David Tudor 128-9
Stravinsky, Igor *The Rite of Spring*
 94
Strauss, Johann entertainment
 music 93-4
Sullivan, Arthur, 'Propior Deo' 81
Supičič, Ivo 15-16

Tchaikovsky, Peter Ilyich Sixth
 Symphony 85
Thoreau, David & Charles Ives
 78, 91
Thomson, Katharine & *Don
 Giovanni* 58
Tudor, David 128-9
 & Stockhausen 128-9
 & Karl Wörner 129

University of Natal &
 improvisation 119-20

Vertov, Dziga the camera 126
Valéry, Paul art & technology
 107-8

Wagner, Richard 93
 Tristan und Isolde 85
 Die Walküre 85

Wangermann, Ernst &
   Freemasons 69
Webern, Anton von &
   experimental music 121
Wishart, Trevor audience
   participation 111
   and Friends, *Sun—Creativity and
   Environment* 111
Wolf, Robert Erich criticism of
   musicology 15-16
Wooldridge, David & Beethoven's
   Fifth Symphony 78
   & Charles Ives 78

Worringer, Wilhelm theory of
   abstraction 6
Wörner, Karl & David Tudor 129

Young, LaMonte *Piano Piece for
   David Tudor No. 1* 124
   *The Tortoise, His Dreams and
   Journeys* 125

Zola, Émile 26